The Asbury Theological Seminary Series in Christian Revitalization Studies

In this study we are honored to pay homage to the Wesleyan Theological Society for fifty years of service to the Wesleyan holiness tradition. Professors Callen and Hoskins present the story of the WTS by working with a team of contributors representing several historical strands of the society over these years. In one sense, publication of the volume in the Pietist and Wesleyan Studies Series brings the Society full circle. From 1989, David Bundy and I coedited this series through Scarecrow Press. Its early intent was to bring into conversation the polarized fields of Pietist and Wesleyan holiness research, which belong to one greater tradition in the history of modern movements of Christian revitalization. Three studies receiving the Smith Wynkoop Award were among the fifty plus titles published in the Series. These three were written by Diane Leclerc, Laurence Wood, and Floyd Cunningham, published between 2002 and 2004.

Since 2005, the Series has been co-published with the new Center for the Study of World Christian Revitalization Movements at Asbury Theological Seminary, through Emeth Press, with Professor Laurence Wood as publisher. Howard Snyder and I launched the Center in collaboration with other Asbury faculty members, as the successor to the previous Wesleyan Holiness Studies Center at Asbury. The intent was to broaden our research to embrace historical and contemporary expressions of Christian revitalization with focus on the Global South and East. This work has proceeded thanks to two successive grants from the Henry Luce Foundation. A second concern of the Center has been to encourage research in Wesleyan holiness studies as part of this larger focus on revitalization. To that end, the Pietist and Wesleyan Studies Series was relocated within the new Asbury Theological Seminary Series in Christian Revitalization Studies, featuring six sub-series, in which Pietist and Wesleyan Studies is a leading component. Since 2005 I have continued service as editor of the Pietist and Wesleyan Studies Series, in this new configuration, as well as general editor of the ATS Series in which it is housed. Our publisher has been Professor Laurence Wood of Emeth Press, At this juncture, more than 50 volumes have appeared in the Series and its antecedents, since 1989.

We present this commemorative volume on the WTS in tribute to its achievements in promoting research in Wesleyan holiness studies for the past half century, and with the anticipation of a coming chapter in continuing and expanding that contribution.

J. Steven O'Malley, General Editor
The Asbury Theological Seminary Studies in Christian Revitalization

Wesleyan Theological Society

The Fiftieth Anniversary Celebration Volume

*The Asbury Theological Seminary Series in
Christian Revitalization Movements in Pietist/Wesleyan Studies*

Barry L. Callen
Steven Hoskins
Editors

EMETH PRESS
www.emethpress.com

Wesleyan Theological Society
The Fiftieth Anniversary Celebration Volume

Copyright © 2015 Barry L. Callen
and Steven Hoskins
Printed in the United States of America on acid-free paper

All rights reserved. No part of this book may be reproduced, or stored in a retrieval system or transmitted in any form or by any means, electronic, mechanical, photocopying, recording, scanning or otherwise, except as permitted by the 1976 United States Copyright Act, or with the prior written permission of Emeth Press. Requests for permission should be ad- dressed to: Emeth Press, P. O. Box 23961, Lexington, KY 40523-3961. http://www.emethpress.com.

Library of Congress Cataloging-in-Publication Data

Wesleyan Theological Society : the fiftieth anniversary celebration volume / Barry L. Callen, Steven Hoskins editors.
   pages cm
   ISBN 978-1-60947-090-6 (alk. paper)
   1. Wesleyan Theological Society. I. Callen, Barry L., editor.
   BX9995.W4W48 2015
   230'.706--dc23
                    2014049910

Contents

Preface / vii

Chapter 1. WTS: An Historical Overview
   William Kostlevy / 1

Chapter 2. Decade One (1965-74)
   Leo G. Cox / 5

Chapter 3. Decade Two (1975-84)
   Donald W. Dayton / 11

Chapter 4. Decades One and Two
   John Merritt / 17

Chapter 5. Decade Three (1985-94)
   Howard A. Snyder / 23

Chapter 6. Decade Four (1995-04)
   Jennifer Woodruff Tait / 29

Chapter 7. Decade Five (2005-14)
   Steven Hoskins / 37

Chapter 8. The Journal and Editors
   Barry L. Callen / 43

Chapter 9. Wisdom of the Presidents
   Barry L. Callen / 49

Chapter 10. Recent Greats of the Tradition
   Barry L. Callen / 61

Appendixes

   A. WTS Presidents and Editors / 119

   B. Host Institutions for WTS Annual Meetings / 123

   C. Smith/Wynkoop Book Award Recipients / 125

   D. Archived WTS Materials / 127

   E. Recent WTS Annual Meetings with Host Institutions and Meeting Themes / 130

Index of Names / 131

Preface

The Wesleyan Theological Society held its first annual meeting at Spring Arbor College in November, 1965. The meeting, which drew about 60 attendees, was actually the culmination of efforts that had begun two years prior in sessions held during a meeting of the Society's parent body, the National Holiness Association. Papers read at various early gatherings that led to the creation of the WTS were published as *Insights into Holiness* (1963) and *Further Insights into Holiness* (1963). These conferences and publications led to the Winona Lake Study Conference on the "Distinctives of Arminian-Wesleyan Theology" held in November, 1964, also sponsored by the NHA. Papers from this conference were published as *The Word and the Doctrine* (1965).

With a rising tide of interest in creating a separate scholarly society dedicated to Wesleyan/Holiness theology, the Wesleyan Theological Society was organized at the April, 1965, NHA meeting in Detroit. By the end of its charter membership drive, the WTS numbered 92 official members coming from the Methodist Church, Church of the Nazarene, United Missionary Church, Free Methodist Church, Wesleyan Methodist Church, and Salvation Army. As the Society now celebrates its fiftieth anniversary, its membership roles exceed 1,000 and its journal, the *Wesleyan Theological Journal*, is one of the more respected scholarly publications. This half-century has been very busy and most significant in advancing scholarship in one of the great theological traditions of Christianity.

The many materials that comprise this volume celebrate the fifty-year history of the Wesleyan Theological Society. They document its many achievements since those first formative meetings and publications. The reader will find in these pages a comprehensive history of the Society's annual meetings, a recounting of its central debates and ecumenical endeavors, along with profiles of its key leaders over the past five decades. The book also features an extensive list of names in its index for the use of the researcher and other interested persons.

We, the editors of this 50th-anniversary history volume of the WTS, have found the entire process a happy endeavor. We are grateful to the Society for its trust in us. We express our thanks to earlier persons whose work is rich in historical detail and interpretation and without whom our work would not have been possible. We are grateful to these historians in particular: William Kostlevy, Leo G. Cox, Donald W. Dayton, John Merritt, Howard W. Snyder, and Jennifer Woodruff Tait. Some of the essays included in this volume first appeared in the pages of the *Wesleyan Theological Journal* and others appear here for the first time.

We are especially appreciative of our publisher, Laurence W. Wood of Emeth Press, for his partnership in this project and willingness to provide copies of this book free of charge to all those attending the 50th-anniversary annual meeting of the WTS convened at Mount Vernon Nazarene University in March, 2015. The commitment of Wood and Emeth Press to this book and others like it have done much over the years to keep Wesleyan/Holiness thinkers and their work at the forefront of academic and pastoral scholarship.

It is our fondest hope that this work will serve both to recount the history of the Wesleyan Theological Society and to provide a pathway into what we believe will be a fruitful future only now beginning to emerge.

—Barry Callen and Steven Hoskins
 Editors, March, 2015

Chapter 1

Wesleyan Theological Society: An Historical Overview

by William Kostlevy

Originally published in the *Holiness Digest* (Spring, 1993) and in the *Wesleyan Theological Journal* (Spring, 1995).

Although not formally organized until 1965, the Wesleyan Theological Society is best understood as one of the more significant products of the evangelical "renaissance" of the 1940s and 1950s. Its founders included scholars of notable accomplishment who, in the two decades following WWII, had written a series of ground-breaking doctoral disser-tations and had founded the first evangelical scholarly journal, the *Asbury Seminarian*.

Particularly noteworthy in the beginning of the Society were a series of conferences in the early 1960s conducted at Wesleyan/Holiness colleges under the leadership of Kenneth Geiger, president of the National Holiness Association. Important papers from these conferences were published by Beacon Hill Press of Kansas City as *Insights into Holiness* (1963) and *Further Insights into Holiness* (1963). These conferences culminated in the Winona Lake Study Conference on the "Distinctives of Arminian-Wesleyan Theology." It was convened in November, 1964, and sponsored by the NHA. Papers from this conference were compiled by Kenneth Geiger and published in 1965 by Beacon Hill Press of Kansas City as *The Word and the Doctrine*.

J. C. McPheeters, the respected elder statesperson of the Holiness Movement, indicated in the 1965 Geiger publication that the Winona Lake conference "was perhaps the most significant event in our gen-

1

eration for the spread of Scriptural holiness." It was this meeting which set the stage for the organization of the Wesleyan Theological Society at the April, 1965 National Holiness Association meeting in Detroit. The stated purpose of the new organization was to encourage an exchange of ideas among Wesleyan/Holiness theologians, develop a source of papers for NHA seminars, stimulate scholarship among young theologians and pastors, and publish a journal containing significant contributions to Holiness Movement scholarship.

Leo Cox of Marion College (now Indiana Wesleyan University) was elected the first WTS president, with Merne Harris of Vennard College, secretary, and W. Ralph Thompson of Spring Arbor College, treasurer. Other early presidents of the WTS were Richard Taylor, William Arnett, Lowell Roberts, Merne Harris, Ralph Perry, George Blackstone, Robert Mattke, Delbert Rose, and Mildred Wynkoop.

In November, 1965, the organization's inaugural meeting at Spring Arbor College drew approximately sixty people. Reflecting the diversity of its parent body, the NHA, papers were presented by members of the Methodist Church, Church of the Nazarene, United Missionary Church, Free Methodist Church, Wesleyan Methodist Church, and the Salvation Army. In January, 1966, when the initial membership drive ended, the organization could claim ninety-two charter members. From its inception the WTS experienced steady membership growth (by 1970 286, increasing to 1,103 in 1982).

Following the adoption of a constitution in 1969, an increased desire was expressed to establish formal ties to the NHA. At its 1970 annual meeting the WTS voted to become an official commission of the NHA. This relationship would be maintained until much later when the NHA, later the called the Christian Holiness Association, would cease to function and the WTS would incorporate independently.

The most noteworthy early achievement of the WTS was the establishment of a scholarly journal, the *Wesleyan Theological Journal*. Inaugurated in 1966, the journal's first editor, Charles Carter (1965-1972), guided the periodical during its difficult formative years. Initially published annually, the WTS *Journal* has been published bi-annually since 1979.

One of the WTS's most meaningful contributions to the broader Wesleyan/Holiness Movement has been the visibility it has afforded the Holiness Movement in scholarly and ecumenical circles. The WTS, through its members, has made significant contributions at the Oxford Institute of Methodist Studies and the John Wesley Institute near Chicago. It also has had a presence at meetings of the American Academy of Religion and since the early 1980s has been represented in the discussions of the Faith and Order Commission of the World Council of Churches.

In 1975, the Society's president, Eldon Fuhrman, suggested that it might be appropriate to include in WTS discussions individuals representing various theological views and traditions. Since 1983 outside representatives, including John Howard Yoder, Albert Outler, Mortimer Arias, Dale Brown, Thomas Oden, and Craig Blaising, have enriched theological discussion at the WTS's annual meetings. In 1980 the noted Methodist scholar Frank Baker expressed the view of many scholars when he noted that the *Wesleyan Theological Journal* was an important sign of the continued vitality of Wesleyan scholarship and that its articles were "well written and carefully documented" and occasionally were of major importance.

Indicative of the WTS's success is that its stated objectives have been largely realized. The organization has provided a forum for theological reflection in the Wesleyan/Holiness tradition, published significant scholarship in the tradition, and has encouraged a generation of young scholars. The encouragement and publication of the work of young scholars has been one of the most significant fruits of the Wesleyan Theological Society. Beginning with the presentation of papers by Kenneth Kinghorn, at the WTS's first conference, and by Jerry Mercer, at its second, the WTS has provided a continuous forum for young scholars.

The most important contribution of the Wesleyan Theological Society has been in the growing theological maturity of the Wesleyan/Holiness Movement. Reflecting the Society's roots in neo-evangelicalism, the scholarly debate in the early years of the WTS was dominated by issues surrounding the biblical basis of Christian perfection and the doctrine of inerrancy. By the mid-1970s the central concern of the Society was the doctrine of the Baptism of the Holy Spirit. Especially noteworthy was an important dialogue between Donald Dayton and Timothy Smith which stimulated some of the most significant scholarship in the Wesleyan/Holiness tradition, and has helped to clarify important issues surrounding the origins and relationship of the Holiness Movement to Pentecostalism. Equally important has been an extended discussion, beginning at the Society's second annual conference, concerning personal and social ethics in the Wesleyan/Holiness tradition. The Society's 1987, 1989, and

1991 annual meetings included important papers on the social views of the Wesleyan/Holiness Movement.

This, I suspect, is merely the beginning of the story. The recent flowering of theological, philosophical, historical, ethical, and biblical scholarship suggests that the Wesleyan/Holiness tradition, the product of the NHA-sponsored camp meetings of the nineteenth century, has a important role to play in the academy of the twenty-first century.

Chapter 2

Wesleyan Theological Society: The First Decade

by Leo G. Cox

Originally published in the
Wesleyan Theological Journal (Spring, 1995).

Fortunately, I do have a few letters I wrote at the time the WTS began. One of these was written to Delbert Rose, then historian of the National Holiness Association (later the Christian Holiness Association), shortly after the first meeting of the WTS. In it, at his request, I gave an account of how the WTS came into being. I will depend much on the facts in this letter.

During the years of 1955-59, I was in the State University of Iowa struggling to complete a master's thesis on "Wesley's Concept of Sin" and a doctoral dissertation on "Wesley's Concept of Perfection." My counselor was a Presbyterian and the Department of Religion head and a very liberal Methodist. He joked about Wesley's heart-warming as likely only a bout of indigestion. The other members of the committee were a Baptist, a Roman Catholic, a liberal Jew, and a Lutheran. The only one who had much of an idea about Christian perfection was the Roman Catholic.

At that time I was pastor of a Methodist Church and had little contact with any of my holiness colleagues. I tried to think through some of the intellectual problems on my own, and often wished for access to a group of Wesleyan scholars. I needed to discuss with someone who knew the holiness message and could help me in my struggle.

Following the completion of my doctoral degree, I attended some of the meetings of the Evangelical Theological Society. In these meetings I found some help, especially in regard to biblical authority and the place of the Word for my theology. But I still needed more help than I found there. The ETS organizational plan did give me some idea of how one might form a society of Wesleyan scholars.

In the early 1960s I became closely associated with the NHA (later the CHA). Merne Harris of Vennard College was Dean of Seminars for the annual convention. He appointed me to be the seminar leader on doctrine. Here I met leaders of the Holiness Movement. The seminars I led were helpful to me, but most of the scholars were either leading other seminars or were back home teaching their classes. I still longed for an opportunity to discuss with a group of holiness scholars. During these years I hinted to several of my professional friends that there was need for a Wesleyan society. They agreed.

In the years 1961-1963 Kenneth Geiger, President of the NHA, organized a series of seminars on holiness and assigned topics to various scholars. These lectures were given on the campuses of seventeen seminaries and colleges. Usually a group of three or four went to each campus. I remember riding in a car to Canada with Dr. Geiger and Dr. Frank Stanger for a seminar. What a discussion we had! These lectures resulted in the publication of two volumes titled *Insights into Holiness* (1962) and *Further Insights into Holiness* (1963).

Then in 1964 Dr. Geiger planned and implemented in Winona Lake, Indiana, a study conference on the subject "Distinctives of Wesleyan-Arminian Theology." A 1965 book titled *The Word and the Doctrine* published by Beacon Hill Press of Kansas City came as a result of this conference. Here is a quote from the Preface:

> The Winona Lake conference was attended by administrators and pastors and representatives from the academic communities of the several denominations and organizations which participate in the National Holiness Association. Invited observers from other evangelical groups were present. More than eighty individuals—uniquely representative, scholarly and objective—shared in this intensive three-day period.

It was in this conference that my wish of 1955-57 finally came to fruition. Here were able scholars meeting together and discussing the very problems I had experienced. I saw then that the only way to preserve such interchange would be in a society and a journal similar to ETS--and what WTS is now. I had spoken to Merne Harris on some earlier occasions about this possibility and did so again at this Study Conference. I approached him about the possibility of getting together and initiating a Wesleyan Theological Society. He was in full agreement with me on the proposal.

Following the Study Conference I sent to Merne Harris copies of the ETS constitution, some of its programs and application blanks, etc. I wrote a letter to him expressing some of the ideas I would like to have incorporated into such a society. Harris prepared an initial report and submitted it to the NHA Executive Board, which approved going ahead with the formation of such an organization.

Merne Harris proceeded with the outlining of the organizational ideas and asked to have an early meeting with me. On my way to Minneapolis on February 13, 1965, he was able to meet me at the O'Hare Airport. In a two-hour meeting we worked on the Prospectus, which he had already drawn up, and prepared it for presentation to the Executive Board of the NHA. This group approved the Prospectus at its meeting following its presentation by Merne Harris. It is easy, therefore, to understand why WTS initially would be tied closely to the NHA.

At the NHA convention in Detroit, April, 1965, the initial meeting of the Wesleyan Theological Society was held in the Statler Hotel. About twenty were present. The Prospectus was presented, slightly revised, and approved as the constitution of the new society. Then the group elected the officers who were to act between the NHA convention and the first annual meeting of the Society. These officers were: Leo G. Cox, president; Merne Harris, secretary; Ralph Thompson, treasurer; and Richard Taylor, president-elect. This new Executive Committee met to discuss the first annual meeting, set its place and date, and plan the program. The date was November 5 and 6, 1965, with the place being Spring Arbor College. Similar November dates would serve the Society well for many years to come. Merne Harris worked hard in developing a mailing list, preparing the program, and writing to key leaders to prepare papers. Ralph Thompson worked hard in making the plans on the campus of Spring Arbor College for the hosting of the Society. They deserve considerable credit for the success of that first annual meeting. One item of interest is that the total cost per person for all the meals was $3.10. Lunch was 40 cents and the banquet was $1.50.

It was difficult to anticipate how many would be present for that first annual Society meeting. We had hoped that there would be at least thirty to forty. As it turned out, the number surpassed our hopes with about sixty present. The interest level was excellent. By then the membership was 49 and the door was left open until January 1, 1966, for other charter members. Ultimately there were 92 charter members. By 1972 there were about 400 members.

One item of interest is that the planners of that first annual meeting believed that the Friday night speaker after the banquet should be an inspirational preacher of holiness rather than a scholarly presentation, and that the service be public. This desire likely grew out of the practices of the NHA. For the first meeting Dr. J. Sutherland Logan, President of Vennard College, was chosen as the speaker. This practice continued for a few years, but soon that evening spot was assigned to the President of the WTS for a presidential address. We early presidents failed to get our special privilege!

As I remember, the first meeting went rather smoothly. One scholar by accident left his prepared paper at home, so fearfully put some ideas together and presented them from memory. His prepared copy was later published in the first *Journal* (Spring, 1966). The papers and discussions were excellent and all felt that it was time well spent. I was thrilled to think that now was happening what for years I had longed for. We who started this learned society wondered how it would sail. The results of the following years would be very satisfying.

One ideal in our minds was that young scholars could present their ideas for testing before a society of scholars who could discuss the concepts, the older helping to guide the younger. There are changes in approach and in terminology that sometimes stump us older minds, but we learn from these younger and brilliant men and women.

The matter of the relation of the WTS to the NHA (CHA) was discussed at length during these early years. It was explained that there was no legal relationship between them, but a very close relationship nonetheless. It was decided at the invitation of the CHA that the WTS be a commission of the NHA (CHA) organization. The Society was asked to provide the speakers and program for the CHA annual convention. These developments were enacted at the Convention in Portland, Oregon, in 1972, and continued for many years.

The publishing of a journal was proposed in the first meeting and an editorial committee was chosen. Dr. Charles Carter was editor from 1965 to 1972 and he set a high goal for the journal. He was assisted by an editorial committee authorized to edit and publish the papers. The financing of the journal was planned and the hope was expressed that the journal would become a vital function of the Society. Robert Mattke, WTS president in 1971-72, said in his president's report to the CHA: "The publication of an annual journal continues to be one of the more significant contributions of the WTS to the Holiness Movement." There was later a suggestion to have a quarterly publication in cooperation with holiness seminaries. An ad hoc committee worked on such for some time, but by 1975 the idea apparently had lost momentum and ceased as a possibility. The practice of publishing two issues of the journal a year came after the first decade.

The thematic tone struck in the first issue of the *WTJ* brought forward two theological points of tension that would occupy the WTS during its early years. These two doctrinal areas focused on the question of the "inerrancy" of Scripture and the baptism with the Holy Spirit in entire sanctification. The former was addressed especially in the first decade of the WTS, with the second more in the next decade. After some rather heated discussions on inerrancy during those early years, Ralph Thompson, in his report to the Society as secretary-treasurer in 1969, gave this conciliatory appeal:

> Considerable discussion has taken place on the subject of Biblical inerrancy. Those who know me best know I tend to take a stand in favor of the doctrine. Many of my brethren do not see the matter as I do; yet they appear to believe as strongly as I do in the inspiration and authority of the Scriptures. I wonder if a position we hold but cannot prove should debar from membership in this Society those whose minds do not operate exactly as ours. Let us be exceedingly careful lest we take any step that will weaken our position with respect to the inspiration and authority of the Scriptures. But if a change in the wording in our doctrinal statement could be made that would protect our position and at the same time respect that of our brethren whose intellectual honesty will not allow them to subscribe to our statement, I recommend that such action be taken.

The matter of inerrancy was also discussed in CHA business meetings. However, the WTS was allowed to go ahead with the discussion and state the results as it saw best. The discussions were quite strong and feelings were high, but at no time was there any desire to lessen the emphasis on the infallibility of the Word ("infallibility" being a broader term not necessarily tied to certain implications of "inerrancy"). The real problem certain Society members had was in regard to the phrase "inerrant in the originals." This they felt could not be proved and contained difficult implications. By 1969 that matter was resolved in a constitution where the wording is "we believe in the plenary-dynamic and unique inspiration of the Bible as the divine Word of God, the only infallible, sufficient and authoritative rule of faith and practice." It is well that, in the Spirit of Christ, this difference of opinion did not divide our Wesleyan theologians into two camps.

In conclusion, let me say that some of my intellectual perplexities have found a degree of satisfaction over the years. To be with students of like mind, seeking for answers, brings a great degree of stability in one's pursuit of truth. But new questions still arise and the journey of one's mind never ends. I thank God for the WTS and the godly thinkers who have touched my life.

Many questions still remain. My next big move will be to heaven where I believe we will be able to see with much clearer vision. For now, the holy pursuit of knowing God in the divine fullness is our task here. May the Wesleyan Theological Society continue to guide young thinkers on the path to Glory, with a clear mind and hearts full of perfect love.

Chapter 3

Wesleyan Theological Society: The Second Decade

by Donald W. Dayton

Originally published in the
Wesleyan Theological Journal (Spring, 1995).

I was elected promotional secretary of the Wesleyan Theological Society in 1975 and served in that office for eleven years. As I have reflected on this task, I have wondered if a theological society goes through stages of development parallel to those of a human being. If there is any parallel, the second decade of the WTS would encompass late childhood, puberty, and adolescence. The metaphor may finally fail, but it strikes me that such an image might well characterize the themes of these years of the second decade. They were awkward years of struggle toward maturity—toward an independent identity in a larger arena of theology and scholarship.

Let me illustrate these dynamics with three themes. I think that you will understand the first better if I indulge in a moment of personal autobiography that illumines a dimension of the development of the WTS.

The "Inerrancy" of the Scriptures

I was born into the Wesleyan Church, one of the wings of the holiness movement most influenced by "fundamentalism"—to the extent of officially embracing the doctrine of the "inerrancy of the Scriptures" that was the identity marker of the "neo-evangelical" movement during the founding years of the WTS. It is no accident that the original organizing committee of the WTS was dominated by Wesleyans. Unfortunately, for a period of years I accepted the fundamentalist logic (that Christian faith is unthinkable without this doctrine). I was prevented from embracing Christianity, let alone Wesleyanism, until I was at Yale Divinity School and there became able to develop an authentically authoritative but non-inerrantist doctrine of Scripture.

During my sojourn at Yale I was invited to a meeting of graduate students that came to be known as the "Rye Conference," even when in later years this meeting was held at the Free Methodist headquarters in Winona Lake, Indiana. In its early years this meeting was somewhat secretively supported by sympathetic figures in Winona Lake who squeezed a little blood out of their budgetary turnips to enable these discussions. I will always honor these Free Methodist leaders for this creative project that was an extraordinary help to many of us then struggling in graduate school.

I will never forget one Rye paper by Frank Thompson of Greenville College. He wept as he agonized over the extent to which the early WTS commitments to the doctrine of inerrancy precluded his (and others!) participation in the theological society of his tradition. The members of the Rye Conference petitioned George Turner of Asbury Theological Seminary to carry to the next WTS meeting a request that this orientation be changed.

I, of course, was not present at the 1969 meeting in Marion, Indiana, and have never been sure whether the reports about this meeting (the tensions, tie votes, etc.) might be apocryphal. But the WTS articles of faith were modified sufficiently in the direction of a doctrine of "infallibility" that I and others took the changes as an invitation to join the Society in the following years. Without these changes I and many others would not be here today. When I reflect on this history, I am astonished that I have had any role in the Society and how close the Society came to having a very different history.

A crucial compromise of that Marion meeting quoted the Random House Dictionary definition of "infallibility"—citing the source as "RHD." These cryptic initials raised many questions in the following years about the nature of this unidentified theological authority. It was not until the end of the seventies that the Society felt free to rid itself of this theological gaucherie, ostensibly for stylistic reasons, but more profoundly and courageously disassociating the Society and its theological tradition from fundamentalism. Melvin Dieter was the WTS president at the time and we debated the issue for some years before agreeing that the executive committee would not make a formal recommendation, but that I could make a motion from the floor. We were all astonished when the motion provoked only minor discussion and only two negative votes.

The "Baptism of the Holy Spirit"

But it was a second issue—the debates about the *Baptism of the Holy Spirit*—that dominated the middle decade of my assignment as the WTS promotional secretary. This war was started with a 1972 shot fired across the Atlantic from Britain by Nazarene pastor Herbert McGonigle. He could not be present, but sent his paper "Pneumatological Nomenclature in Early Methodism" that puzzled over the lack of "pentecostal" vocabulary in the Wesleys (see *WTJ*, Spring, 1973). At the time I was working on nineteenth-century Oberlin Perfectionism in my doctoral studies at the University of Chicago. Prompted by McGonigle, I thought I had found the hinge of this transition in mid-19th century holiness currents. I presented my conclusions in my first WTS paper in 1973 on Asa Mahan of Oberlin College (*WTJ*, Spring, 1974).

With this essay, the "theology hit the fan" and created some explosions behind the scenes that occasionally broke into the open. The 1974 *WTJ* issue arrived in Taiwan where Charles Carter was reading the proofs of a book on the Holy Spirit that reflected the late nineteenth-century developments and had already been endorsed by the Christian Holiness Association. My essay was attacked in a two-page footnote added to the galleys. I felt compelled to respond in a review of Carter's book in *Christianity Today*. About this time Timothy Smith joined the fray, and the war was on. Behind the scenes caucuses of the leadership of the CHA and others raised the specter of church splits and the theological collapse of the tradition. The motives of scholars on both sides of the question were impugned, and many wondered if we could emerge from these debates unscathed. The issues came to a head in the 1977 and 1978 Society meetings, then they soon subsided without any clear resolution.

I have always thought this debate was very important in the life of our Society—completely apart from any resolution of the issues. To me it revealed the genius of the WTS and the importance of our continuing to do our work *together*. It has always seemed to me that the Nazarenes have done better, by leading us beyond the debates about the doctrine of Scripture, than have the often-paralyzed Wesleyans and Free Methodists. The Nazarene's history of isolation from fundamentalism (perhaps from "sectarian" motives) allowed them to finesse the issues involved, while they found themselves more threatened by the "pneumatological nomenclature" debates that were not so threatening to the Wesleyans and Free Methodists, whose identities were less shaped by the late nineteenth-century developments.

More important, if I had any reason for pushing this debate, it was because of my intuition that it would advance our own theological maturity by raising questions from within rather than from without the tradition. This issue raised some very important questions that challenged our biblicism about various issues and raised significant questions about the development of doctrine. We are a movement with two generating moments—one in the Wesleyanism of the 18th century and one in the holiness movement of the 19th century. These are not entirely congruent, and our struggle with these differences may help free us to face the challenges of articulating the Wesleyan message into the 20th and 21st centuries. We cannot meet these challenges by repeating the clichés of either the 18th or 19th centuries.

Use of "Outside" Speakers

A final issue may seem on the surface to be trivial, but I am convinced that it serves as a measure of our theological self-confidence and willingness to engage in wider dialogue. The issue arose in the midst of the battles over the "baptism with the Spirit." Charles Carter returned from Taiwan. I proposed that he chair the nominating committee, and the report of his committee became a test of the future direction of the Society. In 1975, at the Society's meeting on the campus of Circleville Bible College, we had some very tense votes. Their deeper significance was whether we would short-circuit the move away from fundamentalism or move back toward it. I remember discovering in that meeting that the Society sometimes would vote one direction on a secret ballot and another in a public voice vote or display of hands.

This became clear to me as we debated the question of whether to invite "outside speakers" to participate in our meetings. My memory is that it was by secret ballot that we accepted in principle an openness to the participation of leaders outside the Wesleyan tradition. In this meeting I made one of my most egregious miscalculations. It seemed to me that we might appropriately invite Vinson Synan of the Pentecostal Holiness Church to give a paper. He had been a member of the Society and had so admired the WTS that he used it in part as a model for the founding of the Society for Pentecostal Studies. I had underestimated the anti-pentecostal animus of the WTS and how it could (and did) create a backlash to this proposal. The negative response was so strong that it would be another eight years before the issue could be seriously broached again.

In 1983, at the Society's meeting on the campus of Anderson University, John Howard Yoder became our first "outside speaker" by responding to a panel exploring the significance of the "restorationist" motif in the holiness movement. The next year we met at Emory University to celebrate the Methodist Bicentennial and heard Albert Outler reflect on the Wesleyan Quadrilateral. Since then we have not always felt compelled to have these outside speakers, but we seem no longer threatened by their appearance—and a number of important scholars and theologians have participated in our work without derailing us.

Such developments seem to me to be signs of growing self-confidence and the maturing of identity in the late adolescence of the Wesleyan Theological Society. Now moving toward middle age, we can look back on this tumultuous WTS decade with more equanimity—but with the realization that it was a decade that set us on our current path. Only time will tell the fuller story of the wisdom of these implicit decisions, but I continue to be encouraged by our theological health and vigor. Sometimes, in the midst of the conflicts, it has been difficult to see our maturation and development—and to celebrate it. Even so, the Society has been precocious in its development—much more precocious than I would have perceived in the years of its childhood.

Chapter 4

Fellowship in Ferment: A WTS History, 1965-1984

by Major John G. Merritt (Salvation Army)

Originally published in the *Wesleyan Theological Journal* (Spring/Fall, 1986). Abbreviated.

Laying the Foundations

The connection with the Christian Holiness Association (CHA) points to the broad context in which the Wesleyan Theological Society was born. It grew from the conviction of five educators in schools and denominations related to the CHA that there was need for a fellowship of scholars in the Wesleyan/Holiness tradition comparable to the Evangelical Theological Society. These men were William M. Arnett (Methodist), Asbury Theological Seminary, Wilmore, Ky.; Leo G. Cox (Wesleyan Methodist), Marion College, Marion, Ind.; Wilber T. Dayton (Wesleyan Methodist), Asbury Theological Seminary; Merne Harris (Wesleyan Methodist), Vennard College, University Park, Iowa; and W. Ralph Thompson (Free Methodist), Spring Arbor College, Spring Arbor, Mich.

These five decided to contact their colleagues in the (then) National Holiness Association (NHA) about the feasibility of such an organization, and if interest was sufficient to launch a learned society during the April, 1965, convention of the NHA/CHA in Detroit, Michigan. The response was positive and thus the meeting was convened. It resulted in the formation of the Wesleyan Theological Society, with Leo G. Cox of Marion College being elected president. It was decided that the first annual meeting of the WTS would be held

November 5-6, 1965, at Spring Arbor College, with the summer and fall being devoted to the securing of charter members. This initial membership effort concluded January 1, 1966, and resulted in a charter membership of ninety-two persons, seventy-nine of which held the B.D., M.A., Th.M., Th.D. or Ph.D. degrees.

The interim executive committee met in Chicago at the Hoyne Avenue Wesleyan Methodist Church in August to plan the program for the first weekend of November, 1965--which set the chronological precedent for subsequent annual meetings of the WTS. The inaugural event was attended by approximately sixty persons, and during the first business meeting of the Society Dr. Cox proposed the possibility of an annual bulletin. After Milton S. Agnew of The Salvation Army and Wilber T. Dayton of Asbury Theological Seminary made suggestions about the financing of the venture, it was decided to refer the matter to the executive committee.

It was further agreed that a new editorial board would have the right to select, edit, and publish papers presented on the conference floor. This inaugural editorial board consisted of Arthur M. Climenhaga (Brethren in Christ), Wilber T. Dayton (Wesleyan Methodist), and Armor D. Peisker (Pilgrim Holiness). The minutes reveal agreement that this was the function of this group. Professor Carter (editor from 1965 to 1972), assisted by the editorial committee, produced the first number of the *Wesleyan Theological Journal* in the spring of 1966. The significance of this publication would be long-term. The journal would become a significant contribution of the Wesleyan Theological Society to the Holiness Movement and beyond.

In a period which overlapped 1978 and 1979 there was particular effort expended to publicize the WTS and the *WTJ* in the two major magazines of American Protestantism, *Christianity Today* and the *Christian Century*. Unfortunately, according to the reporting of Donald Dayton, WTS promotion secretary, the efforts were not always met with gratifying results. Professor Dayton's promotional efforts in other directions were more rewarding in the making of positive contacts with and participation in the Oxford Institute of Methodist Studies in England and the John Wesley Theological Institute near Chicago.

There also was a WTS display at a meeting of the American Academy of Religion/Society of Biblical Literature in a joint venture with other evangelical scholarly journals. The *WTJ* was the only journal featured which was Wesleyan-Arminian in orientation. Dayton noted this in his 1984 report to the WTS:

> In the last few years I have been drawn into certain ecumenical discussions where I have been able to represent the WTS and the CHA constituency to some extent. In this process I have discovered the alarming extent to which we are not even on the intellectual map of many church leaders. We tend to be lost amongst the Evangelicals or confused with the Pentecostals. We have only recently, for example, begun to be counted among the "world confessional bodies."

Although Dayton's comments focused on the need for the WTS to move out into and be correctly recognized by the larger ecclesiastical world, a converse concern was indicated as far back as 1975 when Eldon Fuhrman, of Wesley Biblical Center and the WTS president that year, raised the question about inviting those of other theological positions to participate in WTS annual meetings. Although the ensuing discussion during the business session revealed mixed reactions, the minutes state that a motion was passed directing the Program Committee to prepare guidelines for bringing scholars of other theological positions. There was, however, clear hesitation about "outside speakers" being published in the Society's journal.

The Precursors of Ferment

Having staked out the organizational parameters in which the Wesleyan Theological Society was born and has matured, we now turn our attention to the thematic tone that was struck in the first issue of the Journal and its implications for the two major theological crises through which the Wesleyan Theological Society has gone and may still be going through. The first number of the *WTJ* occupies more than an obviously historical place in the WTS; it also enjoys a seminal status in the theological witness and movement of the Society. This proposition is rooted in the fact that the first number contains some of the more basic and distinctive emphases of the Wesleyan/Holiness Movement.

The lead article of the first *WTJ* issue in 1966 was "Entire Sanctification as Taught in the Book of Romans" by Wilber T. Dayton. His interpretive approach set a hermeneutical tone and interfaced with the exegetical basis suggested for the various aspects of the Wesleyan understanding of holiness that spin off from the crucial term of "entire sanctification." At the time there was a fear of a decreasing emphasis on the Wesleyan doctrine of perfect love. Thus, we may ask this question. Although the expressed purpose of the founding of the Society was the creation of a forum for the scholarly study and presentation of the doctrine of Christian perfection as understood by John Wesley, was there implicitly present also the purpose of preserving, on a scholarly basis, a doctrine that was perceived to be receiving diminishing emphasis in the Holiness churches?

Kenneth Geiger, then general superintendent of the United Missionary Church, commences his paper on "The Biblical Basis for the Doctrine of Holiness" with a reference to the inerrancy of the original autographs of Scripture, stating that this is "the official position of the National Holiness Association and, quite uniformly, the view of Wesleyan-Arminians everywhere. "This unequivocal pronouncement causes us to wonder if Geiger was speaking too emphatically and generally since developments within the first three years of the founding of the WTS point away from such universality of agreement regarding Scripture. The WTS would later remove from its doctrinal statement the reference to Scripture as "inerrant in the originals."

Milton S. Agnew's discussion of "The Works of the Holy Spirit," particularly in the section dealing with the relation of Pentecost to holiness and purity, doubtless is a precursor of the intense and varied understandings of that connection in Wesley's theology. Differences of understanding surfaced dramatically in the *WTJ* between 1978 and 1980. If these observations—made in light of the total historical context of the *WTJ*—are correct, then even in the first meeting of the Society and in the inaugural issue of its journal we already see emerging the two concerns which eventually would become the most important areas of critical discussion thus far in the existence of the WTS and the *WTJ*.

The Ferment Erupts--Thematic Directions

How did the thematic tone set in the first issue of the *Wesleyan Theological Journal* work out in the subsequent numbers? We see the articles in volume 1 (Spring 1966) through volume 19 (Spring 1984) falling--sometimes in an overlapping way—under twelve basic rubrics, namely: John Wesley himself, distinctive Wesleyan emphases on holiness, Scripture, the Holy Spirit, the Wesleyan Movement and Evangelicalism, the theological roots of Wesleyanism, practical theology, philosophical issues, contemporary theology, Wesleyan perspectives on various doctrines and theological disciplines, historical issues, and miscellaneous topics. I have traced all of these articles by these twelve categories, their writers, the writers' denominations, the schools represented by the writers, and the distribution of each category by the decade of the *WTJ*'s publication from 1966 through 1984.

This thematic and writer overview provides the larger framework within which to pinpoint the two areas which have been the most crucial in the history of the WTS: (1) the problem of biblical inerrancy/infallibility and (2) the debate over the relation of the expression "baptism with the Holy Spirit" to the central Wesleyan distinctive of "entire sanctification." As proposed above, both controversies were anticipated — no doubt without design — in the seminal, inaugural issue of the *WTJ* in the spring of 1966, and periodically they have surfaced in varying degrees of intensity throughout the publishing history of the journal.

[Merritt proceeds to explain in some detail the thematic directions that erupted, highlighting especially (1) the problem of the nature of Scripture and (2) the problem of expressing the doctrine of entire sanctification in pneumatological language. Some of this information may be found in this book in the chapter on the history of the *Wesleyan Theological Journal*.]

Summary and Conclusion

In summarily comparing the two major doctrinal crises which the Wesleyan Theological Society has encountered in the first twenty years of its history, we may make at least two observations. (1) The first crisis, regarding Scripture, was a philosophical one with historical overtones and theological consequences. (2) The debate over the relation of Spirit baptism to Christian perfection was a hermeneutical one — both biblically and historically — which bore profound theological significance for the Wesleyan/Holiness tradition in North America. But, as disturbing as these debates and controversies may have been to the constituency of the WTS and the readers of the *WTJ*, they are empirical evidence for the general assessment that the WTS soon became a primary venue for mediating the theological ferment that has marked the current study of John Wesley and the variegated movement that bears his name.

Ken Collins and Larry Wood

Chapter 5

Wesleyan Theological Society: The Third Decade

by Howard A. Snyder

Originally published in the
Wesleyan Theological Journal (Spring, 1995).

The Wesleyan Theological Society never has existed in a vacuum. From its beginning it has reflected influences of the larger church and society. So it also has been during the Society's third decade. The Society's history continues to be marked by a variety of external and internal pressures. In these brief reminiscences of these ten years I want to mention three transitions in the life of this theological community.

From Wesleyan-Arminian to Wesleyan-Holiness

The Wesleyan Theological Society was formed officially as "A fellowship of Wesleyan-Arminian scholars." Often the term was hyphenated "Wesleyan-Arminian," indicating a kind of equal weight between the two terms: To be Wesleyan was to be Arminian. In the last five years the Society increasingly has described itself as "Wesleyan/Holiness" or "Wesleyan Holiness" rather than "Wesleyan-Arminian." Why?

The change from "Wesleyan-Arminian" to "Wesleyan/Holiness" occurred officially with the constitutional revision adopted in 1991. Previously the first item of the Bylaws' "Purpose" section had read, "To encourage an exchange of ideas among Wesleyan-Arminian scholars...." This was changed in 1991 to read, "To promote theological interchange among Wesleyan/holiness scholars...." This change has been reflected on the front of the annual program brochure since 1992.

What kind of shift in self-consciousness is suggested by this seemingly minor word change? It seems to signal two things. First, it is a shift from a more theological to a more historical emphasis. Or, to quote from the 1994 WTS presidential address of George Lyons, it is perhaps evidence that "We have become more descriptive than normative" in our theological work.

In the early days of WTS, the important thing was to understand, articulate, and defend a theological perspective (seen to be vital to the church's integrity and vitality). Increasingly the task became seen as describing historically and reviewing critically the Wesleyan theological tradition, especially in its North American embodiments, with some degree of inter-action with other traditions and the various academic disciplines. Increasingly, Wesleyan scholars (at least those represented at WTS) have come to see themselves more as heirs of a particular tradition (the nineteenth-century Holiness Movement) than as defenders of a particular theological system.

Second, and relatedly, the shift from "Arminian" to "Holiness" signaled a growing theological and historical awareness that John Wesley's theology is not to be defined primarily in terms of an Arminian-Calvinist polarity, but in a much more multi-faceted way. Further, Arminius himself should not be seen as the polar opposite of John Calvin or Calvinism. For most WTS members today, it seems that "Wesleyan-Arminian" has the feel of past controversies, while "Wesleyan Holiness" locates one better on today's ecclesiastical landscape.

From Exclusiveness to Inclusiveness

A second tendency discernible over the past decade has been a gradual move from exclusiveness to inclusiveness in certain areas. Since "exclusive" is often taken negatively and "inclusive" positively (or vice versa), I hasten to add that I am speaking descriptively, not evaluatively. This shift is, of course, related to the developments I mentioned above. It is easier to be inclusive if one is simply describing, not defending.

In its early years, WTS was almost exclusively composed of scholars, pastors, and denominational leaders representing the smaller Wesleyan/Holiness denominations, plus United Methodists associated with Asbury Theological Seminary—all the direct heirs of the

Holiness Movement. The doctrinal statement and membership requirements were more exclusive than they are now. The Society never met at United Methodist seminaries. In its thirty-year history, WTS has rarely met at any of the official United Methodist seminaries. Coincidentally, these exceptions occurred on the Society's twentieth and thirtieth anniversaries: at Emory University (Candler School of Theology) in 1984 and at United Theological Seminary in 1994.

In several respects WTS has become more inclusive over this past decade. The most obvious, and structurally the most significant sign of this shift was the Society's constitutional revision adopted in 1991. For comparison, see the WTS Bylaws in the *WTJ* (Spring, 1990), 157-62, and (Fall, 1990), 125-30. The key changes were (1) the adoption of the Christian Holiness Association's statement of faith, in place of the previous WTS Doctrinal Statement, (2) the addition of "Affiliate Member" and deletion of "Associate Member" categories, and (3) the discontinuation of the Membership Committee.

The principal effects of these changes were (1) to open membership in the Society to those "who are interested in the work of the Society but do not wish to become full members," whether for doctrinal or other reasons, and (2) to make the level of membership more a matter of individual choice than of the Society's rules. More subtly, these changes also made membership in the Society more a matter of identification with a tradition than of creedal commitment.

The broadening of the Society during the past decade is seen also in the names of guest lecturers or presenters, including Mortimer Arias, Dale Brown, Theodore Jennings, Canon Alchin, and Craig Blaising. Another significant example of increasing inclusiveness is the growing openness toward Pentecostal scholars. At one time, even to invite a Pentecostal to speak at WTS was highly controversial. Now a few Pentecostals are members of our Society, one of our members has served consecutively as president of the Society for Pentecostal Studies and president of WTS (Donald Dayton, 1988-90), and we are considering a possible joint meeting between WTS and SPS.

Thus, the circles of WTS have widened in several respects. In part this reflects the broadening interests of WTS members. It also reflects the growing penetration of Wesleyan/Holiness scholars into ecumenical and interdenominational forums. Included are the official or quasi-official involvement of WTS in the Oxford Institute of Methodist Theological Studies (1987 and 1992, and earlier), the WCC Faith and Order discussions (going back to the 1980s), the Wesleyan/Holiness Women Clergy Conference (1994) and, more informally, the Society for Pentecostal Studies and the AAR/SBL in its Wesley Studies section. To date this growing inclusiveness is not much reflected in the ethnic and gender composition of the Society.

From the Church to the Academy

A third trajectory of the Society's movement seems to be from the church to the academy. WTS increasingly has become a creature of the academy and less of the church. I do not mean that earlier leaders and participants in WTS were not scholars, nor that today's WTS scholars are not significantly church related. That would be untrue. I simply mean that the concerns, presentations, and even procedures of the Society are increasingly those of the academy—the secular academy, in fact—rather than of the church in its historic Wesleyan expressions. For example, it is curious how we can now speak of "the Christ event," a passive construction, when referring to God's acts in the life, death, and resurrection of Jesus. This is a sign of how modern and postmodern sensibilities creep into our language and thinking without our even being aware of it.

My impression also is that the content and methodological focus of WTS meetings increasingly reflect the concerns of the academy rather than those of the church. This is probably to be expected, and is not necessarily bad. But it does mean that the WTS runs the risk of overlooking or ignoring crucial issues of church life and experience. Here are two examples:

> 1. With a few notable exceptions, WTS has never seriously and substantively addressed the subject of ecclesiology. For the most part, the Society has bypassed both biblical and Wesleyan understandings of the church, with only seven articles in the *WTJ* during 1985-95 being ecclesiological in the broad sense. This bypassing has been especially true over the past ten years. Perhaps this tendency reflects the individualism of North American culture as much as it does the biases of the academy. Papers that deal with or mention sanctification assume that the discussion is about individual believers, not about Christian community and mutual accountability. We thus show ourselves to be the heirs of the nineteenth-century Holiness Movement more than of early Methodism.
>
> 2. With regard to the interpretation of Scripture, WTS has paid scant attention to Wesley's conception of the "analogy of faith." Wesley neither developed "a canon within the canon" nor split up history and doctrine within Scripture. Wesley's use of "the analogy of faith" may be understood as interpreting all of Scripture in terms of the main historical story line of the redemption that God has accomplished through Jesus Christ. We are to interpret Scripture according to "the analogy of faith" (Rom. 12:6), that is as Wes-

ley says in his *Explanatory Notes on the New Testament*, "according to that grand scheme of doctrine which is delivered [in Scripture], touching original sin, justification by faith, and present, inward salvation. There is a wonderful analogy between all these; and a close and intimate connexion between the chief heads of that faith 'which was once delivered to the saints.' Every article, therefore, concerning which there is any question should be determined by this rule; every doubtful scripture interpreted according to the grand truths which run through the whole."

Clearly, the agenda of our discussions has been and must be set in part by the issues of the day. But I raise these examples to highlight the question of whether we are responding to the issues of the academy or to those of the church, and how we best negotiate between or integrate the two.

If there is in fact such a shift from the church to the academy, perhaps it is reflected in attendance at WTS gatherings. Though I have no confirming statistics, my impression is that a higher number of pastors and non-academic denominational leaders attended WTS meetings ten or fifteen years ago than is true today. WTS meetings were a place where pastors could get some theological updating and even some inspiration. This is still true to some extent, but the tendency appears to be to have more papers on increasingly technical subjects requiring academic expertise, with less time for informal discussion, worship, and singing.

In summary, the Wesleyan Theological Society over the past ten years has continued a gradual, perhaps inevitable transition. Partly, it has been the continuation of developments in the earlier periods of the Society's history; partly the transition has come in response to new challenges. The Society seems to be in a good position to enter its fourth decade and make a useful contribution to both the church and the larger academic community.

Douglas Strong and Randy Maddox

Chapter 6

Wesleyan Theological Society: The Fourth Decade, 1995-2005

by Jennifer L. Woodruff Tait

Not previously published.

When the Wesleyan Theological Society celebrated its thirtieth anniversary in 1995, it could justly claim that its stated goals had been largely realized. It had provided a forum for theological reflection in the Wesleyan/Holiness tradition, published significant scholarship in the tradition, and had encouraged a new generation of young scholars. What next? On the occasion of that thirtieth anniversary, Howard Snyder reflected in the *Wesleyan Theological Journey* about the Society's third decade (1985-1995), saying that during that decade it had moved in three directions: from defining itself as Wesleyan-Arminian to Wesleyan-Holiness, from exclusiveness to inclusiveness, and from church to academy.

To some degree, those moves were also characteristic of the Society's fourth decade—with, perhaps a little tweaking. The first was from centering on being Wesleyan-Holiness to simply proclaiming itself as Wesleyan. The second is a parallel inclusion-exclusion move: as the Society attempted to (and to some degree did) become more diverse in race and gender, it became denominationally less diverse. The third, the move from church to academy, can stand for the fourth decade as it did for the third.

New Leaders and Relationships

The 30th WTS anniversary celebrated in 1995 represented not only a looking-back but a looking-forward, inaugurating several things which were to characterize the Society for years to come. Of primary importance was that the editorship of the *Wesleyan Theological Journal* passed from Paul Bassett to Barry Callen who would carry this central Society role until at the 2014 meeting.

Also, the first Lifetime Achievement Award (named at that point as an award for "lifetime service to the Wesleyan/Holiness tradition") was presented to Robert A. Traina, Professor Emeritus of Biblical Studies at Asbury Theological Seminary. The award had been proposed at the 1993 meeting by then-president Don Thorsen. The presidential address was given by George Lyons, "Biblical Theology and Wesleyan Theology." The meeting was held at United Theological Seminary (Dayton, OH), a United Methodist institution.

In 1994, though not directly founded by the Wesleyan Theological Society, an organization came into being which would continue to relate to WTS informally and serve as an incubator of female Wesleyan-Holiness leadership and scholarship—the Wesleyan/Holiness Women Clergy that held its first "Come to the Water" conference in Glorietta, New Mexico, April 14-17, 1994. Founder of the WHWC was Susie C. Stanley who had previously served as WTS president (1992-1993). The organization was supported by thirteen holiness colleges and seminaries and by five holiness denominations (Church of God-Anderson, Church of the Nazarene, Free Methodist Church, Wesleyan Church, and Evangelical Friends.) Sermons from that inaugurating conference were later published in the book *Honoring God's Call*. The WHWC has continued to the present day to meet every other year, often issuing a publication in conjunction with the meeting, and their meetings have always been endorsed and promoted by WTS.

Northwest Nazarene University in Nampa, Idaho, was the site of the Society's 1995 annual meeting that considered the theme "Sanctification and the New Creation." At this meeting, the Constitution and Bylaws were revised (the revised version is printed in the *WTJ* 32:1 [1997]) and an endowment fund was created for the Society to enhance scholarship and support scholars in the Wesleyan-holiness tradition. The lifetime award was given to James Earl Massey and the presidential address by Donald A. D. Thorsen was on "Reuniting the Two So Long Disjoined: Knowledge and Vital Piety."

The 1996 annual meeting, with the theme "The Worship of God," was held in Washington, D.C. at Wesley Theological Seminary (the last time WTS would be held at a United Methodist institution until 2008). The presidential address was by Kenneth J. Collins on "The New Birth, John Wesley's Doctrine" and the lifetime award was presented to Melvin Easterday Dieter.

The Society returned to Ohio for its 1997 annual meeting around the theme "Facing the Future: Wesleyan/Holiness Theological Resources for the 21st Century." The site was Mt. Vernon Nazarene College University (where the Society would return in 2015 for its fiftieth-year celebration). The presidential address was on "Uniting Worship, Preaching, and Theology" by Wesley Tracy and the lifetime award was given to William Greathouse. Clark Pinnock served as a guest keynote speaker, beginning a tradition picked up in later years of inviting a distinguished theologian or philosopher who was not necessarily a member of WTS to speak to the membership. Editor Barry Callen became personally acquainted with Pinnock at this meeting, leading to his authoring Pinnock's intellectual biography (*Journey Toward Renewal* published in 2000 by Evangel Publishing in cooperation with the WTS).

The 1998 the WTS annual meeting was a groundbreaking one. It represented the Society's first joint meeting with the Society for Pentecostal Studies. As Barry Callen wrote in *WTJ* 34:1 (1999), "In 1993 two Christian leaders, one from each of these traditions [Wesleyan-holiness and Pentecostal], met in an ecumenical gathering in Spain. Cheryl Bridges Johns was then president of the Society of Pentecostal Studies and Susie Stanley was president of the Wesleyan Theological Society. From their new acquaintance and openness to the moving of God, and from the crucial work and relationships of D. William Faupel, there emerged the proposal for a joint meeting of these two academic societies." The WTS broke its long pattern of annual meetings in November of each year, in part to co-ordinate with the SPS pattern of meeting in March—a custom it has followed ever since. The 1998 joint meeting was held at the Church of God Theological Seminary in Cleveland, TN (now Pentecostal Theological Seminary) with the common theme "Purity and Power: Revisioning the Holiness, Pentecostal and Charismatic Traditions." WTS gave the lifetime award to David Seamands; SPS gave its lifetime award to R. Hollis Gause. The tributes to both men and a select papers in common were presented in both the *WTJ* and *Pneuma*.

That same year psychology faculty members from three institutions (Point Loma Nazarene University, Fuller Seminary, and Eastern Nazarene College) met under the patronage of the Wesleyan Center for Twenty-First Century Studies at Point Loma and organized the Society for the Study of Psychology and Wesleyan Theology.

Also that year, the Society made its first appearance in cyberspace with a page on the website of the Christian Holiness Partnership (formerly the Christian Holiness Association). The page listed only a postal mailing address and the group's mission statement: "The Society's mission is to encourage exchange of ideas among Wesleyan-Holiness theologians; to develop a source of papers for CHP (Christian Holiness Partnership) seminars; to stimulate scholarship among younger theologians and pastors; and to publish a scholarly journal."

Growth from Year to Year

In 1999 "Wesleyan Theology in a Postmodern Era" returned WTS to a Nazarene institution, this time Southern Nazarene University (Bethany, OK), meeting March 5-6. At that meeting, the annual Smith-Wynkoop book award was established, named in honor of two famed contributors to Wesleyan-holiness scholarship, historian Timothy L. Smith and theologian Mildred Bangs Wynkoop. The statement establishing the award named it as honoring "a full-length work published by a recognized academic press...deemed to make a substantive contribution to the author's particular field of study and to the Wesleyan/Holiness tradition generally." The presidential address was by Doug Strong on "Sanctified Eccentricity: The Continuing Relevance of the Nineteenth-Century Holiness Paradigm," and the lifetime award was given to J. Kenneth Grider. That year, for the first time, issues of the journal began to appear online on the website of what was then Northwest Nazarene College under the name *The Wesley Center Online* (www.wesley.nnu.edu), with a five-year embargo between publication and online access.

The annual conference held in 2000 took the theme "The Holy Trinity" and met at Azusa Pacific University and the presidential address by Al Truesdale titled "Holy Love vs. Eternal Hell: The Wesleyan Options." That year brought several firsts. Delbert Rose and Susan Schultz Rose were honored with the lifetime award; Susan Schultz Rose was the first woman to be so honored, and it was the first year the award acquired its current title of "lifetime achievement" rather than "lifetime service." The first Smith-Wynkoop book award was also presented, to Doug Strong's *Perfectionist Politics*. Finally, during that meeting WTS members Brint Montgomery, Thomas Jay Oord, and Robert Thompson began planning for what would eventually become the Wesleyan Philosophical Society.

In 2001 the annual meeting convened at Indiana Wesleyan University and centered around the theme "The Dynamics of Power in the Service of Reconciliation." The Smith/Wynkoop Book Award was presented to William J. Abraham's *Canon and Criterion in Christian*

Theology (Clarendon Press) and the Lifetime Achievement Award was presented to David Loren McKenna. Steve McCormick delivered a presidential address on "Heresies of Love: Toward a Spirit-Christ Ecclesiology." Sometime around 2001 the Society also acquired a more extensive website on the site of Garrett-Evangelical Theological Seminary's Wesleyan and Evangelical Studies program (www.wesleyanforum.org/wts/).

The 2002 annual meeting considered "Mission in The Wesleyan Traditions" and placed WTS back in dialogue with the more conservative side of its heritage by meeting at Hobe Sound Bible College in Florida. At this meeting, WPS met in conjunction with WTS for the first time, and SSPWT sponsored a psychology track and decided to meet at future conferences in conjunction with WPS on the day before the regular Society meeting. The Smith/Wynkoop award went to Diane Leclerc for *Singleness of Heart: Gender, Sin, and Holiness in Historical Perspective* and the lifetime award to A. Wingrove Taylor. Sharon Clark Pearson delivered the presidential address.

WTS's growing commitment to diversity and globalization led the Society to co-sponsor in January, 2003, a special meeting celebrating the 300th anniversary of John Wesley's birth. It convened in Nassau, Bahamas, along with the Bahamas' Wesleyan Fellowship, spearheaded by WTS member Carl Campbell and *WTJ* editor Barry Callen. The theme was "Faith Working Through Love: Wesleyan Traditions Today." An excellent report by David Bundy appears in *WTJ* 38:2 [2003], 251-257). He wrote: "It was perhaps the most ecumenical gathering of the Methodist family ever held. There were representatives of the Anglican Church, the Methodist Church of the Bahamas, Methodist Church of the Caribbean and the Americas, independent Methodist congregations, the African Methodist Episcopal Church, the African Methodist Episcopal Zion Church, the Church of the Nazarene, the Free Methodist Church, the Wesleyan Church, the Church of God (Cleveland), and Church of God of Prophecy, Church of the Brethren, Church of God (Anderson), the Baptists, the United Church of Belgium, the Methodist Church of Mexico, and the United Methodist Church (U.S.A.). This historic and unprecedented diversity and participation of Wesley's children, grandchildren, and great-grandchildren united in worship of God, honoring Wesley, singing Methodist hymns, all auguring well for the future of the tradition."

Two months later on March 20-22, 2003, the WTS again met jointly with the SPS in Lexington and Wilmore, KY, in a meeting sponsored by Asbury Theological Seminary. The common theme was

"Wesleyan and Pentecostal Movements for a New Century: Crucial Choices, Essential Contributions." Appropriately, Laurence Wood's *The Meaning of Pentecost in Early Methodism* won the Smith/Wynkoop Book Award. Charles Edwin Jones was given the lifetime award, and the presidential address by David Bundy was on "Visions of Sanctification: Themes of Orthodoxy in the Methodist, Holiness, and Pentecostal Traditions." That same year *Sociedad Wesleyana* (Hispanic Wesleyan Society) was founded, a group interested in promoting Hispanic theological education in the Wesleyan tradition. They would met at WTS—like WPS and SSPWT, on the day before the regular meeting--from 2004-2008. The Korean Wesleyan Society also met in conjunction with WTS from 2003-2007.

In 2004, WTS traveled to upstate New York to the Free Methodist institution of Roberts Wesleyan College and its newly-minted seminary, Northeastern Seminary. William Abraham delivered a keynote which would continue echoing through scholarly discussions for years. It was titled "The End of Wesleyan Theology" (see *WTJ* 40:1 [2005]) and Henry Knight III gave his presidential address on "Realism, Hope, and Holiness in the Wesleyan Tradition." Floyd Cunningham received the Smith/Wynkoop award for his book *Holiness Abroad: Nazarene Missions in Asia* and H. Ray Dunning received the lifetime award. That year, under the leadership of promotional secretary Thomas Oord, the WTS website expanded considerably and moved to Northwest Nazarene University's Wesley Center Online—already hosting the *Journal*—where it would reside for almost a decade.

In May of 2004 the Wesleyan-Holiness Study Project began, with a founding meeting in southern California involving 28 representatives of seven holiness denominations. Each of these denominations committed both funds and scholarly leadership to the project in the hope of producing academically and popularly oriented publications that would create "a renewal in the passion of our pastors and people in preaching and living a thoughtful life of holiness." See the *WTJ* 40:1 [2005], 265-268. The group released a *Holiness Manifesto* in 2006 and in 2011 established Aldersgate Press with Barry Callen elected its Editor (while yet Editor of the *WTJ*). Also supported by many members of the WTS through the years is what began as the Wesleyan Holiness Studies Center at Asbury Theological Seminary in 1991 and is now the Center for the Study of World Christian Revitalization Movements.

Ending the Fourth Decade

The Wesleyan Theological Society ended its fourth decade with its largest attendance to date for the 40th anniversary annual meeting, March 3-5, 2005, at Seattle Pacific University. The theme was "Working Out the Body and Blood of Christ on the 8th Day of Creation." Stanley Hauerwas delivered a keynote address on "The End of Protestantism and the Methodist Contribution" and Phil Meadows delivered the presidential address, "Wesleyan Theology in a Technological Culture." Discussions at that meeting led to the establishment of the WTS dissertation award and the pastor/preacher/scholar award (both would be given for the first time in 2006).

The 2005 Smith/Wynkoop Award went to Samuel Powell's *Participating in God*, and Richard Taylor, the Society's first president, was honored with the lifetime award. In his acceptance speech, he noted, "The holiness movement desperately needs the Wesleyan Theological Society. We began the society to combat the folk theology we found rampant in churches. We wanted to promote issues of the intellect to balance issues of the heart."

The second global meeting endorsed by WTS was in May, 2005, at Seoul Theological University in Seoul, South Korea, on the theme "Wesley, Holiness, and Culture: Trans-Pacific Perceptions for the 21st Century." The *WTJ* 40:2 [2005] reported: "Participants will long remember the tour of historic Korean church sites arranged and directed by Myung Soo Park that included visits to the burial grounds of early western missionaries, the Korea Christian Historical Museum, the historic first church of Korean Methodism, the Korean Salvation Army headquarters, and the Kilbourne Memorial Church located on the old campus of STU."

Throughout this fourth decade, the Society continued to welcome young scholars (something it had done since its first days when the young scholars in question were Kenneth Kinghorn and Jerry Mercer—now among the tradition's elder statesmen!) William Kostlevy served faithfully as the Society's secretary-treasurer from 1992-2005. Such faithful servants helped to keep the Society functional across these years. At the end of its fourth decade, the Society was still very much committed to being a Wesleyan witness to the modern world. It was also increasingly becoming a place where members of certain traditions could discuss issues related to science and faith and postmodern society and theology in ways not comfortable for many within denominations that were focusing more on church growth and being assimilated into generic American evangelicalism.

By the mid-2000s, the Society was well established as a forum for serious academic discussion and debate. How it was to relate practically to the churches was a stickier question. Even if the holiness movement did not recognize (if it ever fully had) that it very much needed the WTS, in Richard Taylor's apt phrase, the WTS entered its fifth decade unsure of something that was equally true—its own need for the holiness movement that had given it birth.

Lane Scott, Donald Dayton, and Don Thorsen

Chapter 7

Wesleyan Theological Society: The Fifth Decade: Broadening Horizons

by Steven Hoskins

Not previously published.

The fifth decade of the Wesleyan Theological Society (WTS) was one of a broadening of horizons. The society's membership grew in greater numbers than ever before and saw an inclusion of scholars from a number of new and renewed theological perspectives and organizations committed to the work of Wesleyan/Holiness theology. With this infusion of new members and perspectives, the boundaries of the of the Society, both literally and figuratively, widened and deepened the Society's service to both the academy and the church as it moved fully into the twenty-first century. The following recollections will illustrate this history as it played out in three trajectories.

A Broader Return to "Pan-Methodist" Roots

The Wesleyan Theological Society was formed in 1965 and officially described itself as "A fellowship of Wesleyan-Arminian Scholars." At its first meeting this concern was reflected in its 92 charter members affiliated with the Methodist Church, Church of the Nazarene, United Missionary Church, Free Methodist Church, Wesleyan Methodist Church, and the Salvation Army. In reality, most of its members came from the ranks of organized and independent Methodist bodies, with some from the smaller holiness bodies found in the middle of that list.

By the time that the society had changed its self-description to read "Wesleyan/Holiness" instead of "Wesleyan-Arminian" in 1991, the majority of its members were from the Church of the Nazarene, with a few scholars from Methodism and other holiness bodies, including the Church of God (Anderson) and some Pentecostal scholars. As its fifth decade proceeded, a clear broadening of the Society's scholarly ranks occurred with a marked increase in total membership, which grew from some 600 members in 2004 to just over a thousand members by 2014.

The broadening of the membership base of the Society in many ways marked a return to the Pan-Methodist membership of the early days of the Society, with new members and new theological concerns coming from some of its earliest parent bodies and a growing number of members coming from schools, churches, and institutions with strong ties and theological commitments to the broader stream of Methodism and holiness theology within the United States. While it is true that "Wesleyan/Holiness" is the better descriptor of the work of the society, the term "Pan-Methodist" better reflects the reach of the Society and its membership by the end of its fifth decade.

Many of the new members came from the ranks of the United Methodist Church, especially those who worked and trained at Duke Divinity School, Asbury Theological Seminary, Perkins School of Divinity at Southern Methodist University, Seattle Pacific University, United Theological Seminary in Dayton, Ohio, Claremont University, and Azusa-Pacific Graduate School of Theology, along with a few scholars from Boston University and Candler School of Theology at Emory University. The upsurge in participation from these Methodist schools certainly reflects their renewed interest in the work of John Wesley and his holiness disciples in the last three centuries, a vigorous and growing branch of theological study which has come into its own in the twenty-first century.

While most of the Society's members came from the Church of the Nazarene and United Methodism during the fifth decade, new membership from other holiness denominations and fellowships also swelled. Included in this increase were members from the Free Methodist Church, Houghton College, the Wesleyan Church, the Salvation Army, and the Church of God (Anderson), all of which had some historical membership ties to the Society. New members were added from the Christian Methodist Episcopal Church, the Brethren in Christ, the African Methodist Episcopal Church, and Evangelical Friends. The number of members from various Pentecostal institutions like the Assemblies of God Seminary in Missouri and Pentecostal Theological Seminary in Cleveland, Tennessee, grew as well.

The growth of Pentecostal members is easily attributed to the continuing joint conferences between the Wesleyan Theological Society and the Society for Pentecostal Studies begun in 1993 and since held every five years. The Society reflected this transformation by holding its annual meetings during the decade at Duke Divinity School (2008), Anderson University (2009), Azusa-Pacific University (2010), Southern Methodist University (2011), and Seattle Pacific University (2013), sites which embraced the renewed "Pan-Methodist" reality of its membership.

A Broader Inclusion of Scholars

With the broadening of the membership to a more Pan-Methodist base during the fifth decade also came to feature a broadening of scholarship within the Society. Clearly the scholarly contributions to the Society's *Wesleyan Theological Journal* and annual meetings were as committed to Wesleyan/Holiness theology and its attending disciplines as in previous decades. However, several new trends emerged as the decade proceeded.

During its fifth decade, leading scholars, both from within the Wesleyan/Holiness bodies and from outside its traditional ranks, were invited to speak to the Society's annual meetings. Prominent scholars such as Walter Brueggemann, Frances M. Young, Jürgen Moltmann, Amos Yong, Christine Pohl, Stanley Hauerwas, I. Howard Marshall, Bruce McCormack, Miroslav Volf, and Society members Randy Maddox, Elaine Heath, and Billy Abraham, addressed the annual meetings on topics reflecting their concerns for theological friendship, suffering, biblical hermeneutics, holiness, and theology and the sciences. Other leading scholars like Michael Cartwright, Dean for Ecumenical & Interfaith Programs at the University of Indianapolis, delivered papers to the meetings that contributed to this broadening of scholarship. The addition of inviting leading scholars to speak at its annual meeting served not only to broaden the thinking done within the Wesleyan/Holiness ranks, but to deepen it as well.

The inclusion of scholars from outside the traditional ranks of the Society was also seen in a number of papers presented at the meetings between 2005-2014. These offerings reflected an ecumenical foment of thought during the decade that broadened participation in the Society's meetings from scholars in the Lutheran, Reformed, and

Roman Catholic traditions, as well as a number of scholars from independent schools like Regent University and Hope International University. Further enriching this ecumenicity were scholars from many of the smaller holiness and Pentecostal bodies like Hobe Sound Bible College in Florida and God's Bible School in Ohio. Clearly, the reach of the WTS, attracting scholars from a wide variety of Christian traditions, only served to strengthen interest in Wesleyan/Holiness scholarship throughout the decade. It should be noted that the essays published during this fifth decade in the Society's *Wesleyan Theological Journal* under the leadership of editor Barry L. Callen, exhibited this new diversity of scholarship. The Society is in debt to the graciousness and ecumenical instincts of its longtime editor.

The most notable broadening of scholars contributing to the Society's meetings during its fifth decade was the participation of a growing number of graduate students. During the years 2005-2014, fully twenty-five percent, one in every four, of the papers presented at the Society's meetings came from students still enrolled in graduate studies, most from the Methodist schools listed above where there was a renewed interest in Wesleyan studies. Encouraging the participation of graduate students, the Society created a new Dissertation of the Year award in 2006. Mark H. Mann, Benjamin L. Hartley, Joanne Cruickshank, Geordan Hammond, Brian Clark, Brent D. Peterson, Patrick Alan Eby, Stanley J. Rodes, and Steven Joe Koskie each won the prize with their dissertation subjects ranging from ecclesiology to science to Wesleyan history.

Another important broadening of the scholarly offerings of the Society came from the ranks of pastoral theologians who helped bridge the gap between academy and church. While the tension between the scholars and the churches and schools they taught in continued throughout the decade, the Society remained committed to its original intention of exploring the Wesleyan witness to the modern world and not building a wall between podium and pulpit. The work of scholars committed to discussing pastoral and ministerial issues in Society meetings helped cement this commitment. The Society wished to be a forum for serious academic discussion and debate about the role of Wesleyan/Holiness theology and its scholars in the church as well as in the academy. This concern was strengthened by the creation of the Pastor-Scholar-Preacher award in 2006, given annually by the Society to those who have made an outstanding contribution to the work of the church outside the academy. Those who won the award during the decade were Brian Postlewait, Jeren Rowell, William Watty, Robert Branson, Robert Luhn, Ronald V. Duncan, Major JoAnn Shade, Dan Boone, Andrew Kinsey, H. Mark Abbott, and Steven Borger. These have served as pastors, superintendents, therapists, and professors, reflecting a broadening of the participation and influence of the Society in both church and academy. At the 2014 meeting, Northwest Nazarene University held its annual pastor's conference in conjunction with the WTS meeting and many of the 100 pastors in attendance attended the WTS meeting as well.

The scholarly societies associated with the Wesleyan Theological Society also made significant contributions to the broadening of scholars and scholarship during the fifth decade. The Korean Wesleyan Society met with the WTS in 2006 and 2007, and throughout the decade the Wesleyan Philosophical Society (WPS), the Wesleyan Holiness/Women Clergy, and the Society for the Study of Psychology and Wesleyan Theology (SSPWT) also met in conjunction with WTS annual meetings. Reflecting the broadening of scholarship from outside the WTS, the 2011 joint meeting of the WPS and the SSPWT invited noted scholar John Caputo of Syracuse University to speak on the theme of suffering. Many of the members of these societies gave papers at the WTS annual meetings as well, with some finding their way into the *Wesleyan Theological Journal*.

In order to better facilitate the broadening of scholarship and the inclusion of more scholars and societies into the work of the Society, the WTS added two significant administrative groups to its committee structure during the decade. Under the leadership of Sam Powell and Thomas Oord, a Consortium of Wesleyan Societies was created to assist the scholarly societies who met in conjunction with the WTS meetings with communication, publicity, and organization of their meetings. Additionally, a Program Units Committee was added to the WTS bylaws to coordinate policies and procedures related to the programs of the annual WTS meetings. This committee assisted the executive officers presiding over meetings and worked with the program unit chairs in putting together the programs for the annual meetings. One goal was creating as diverse a representation of scholars as possible.

A Broader Horizon of Scholarship for Church and Context

The inclusion of a broader range of scholars and scholarship committed to both traditional Wesleyan theological themes and the inclusion of themes dedicated to the emerging theological contexts within which Wesleyan/Holiness scholarship is done was a hallmark of the Society's work during its fifth decade. The history of the WTS between 2005-2014 lends a deeper meaning to the term "Pan-Methodist," one that signifies a responsible allegiance to the study of Wesleyan/Holiness theology and pushes its boundaries into new arenas of theological concern with academic integrity, pastoral devotion, and concern for the world to which it ministers.

The themes of the annual meetings reflect these purposes and the broadening interests of the Society as well. Each of the annual meeting themes--Friendship and Hospitality (2006 at Nazarene Theological Seminary), Suffering (2007 at Olivet Nazarene University), Theology and Society (2008, the joint meeting with The Society for Pentecostal Studies at Duke University), Christology (2009, at Anderson University), The Future of Scripture (2010, at Azusa-Pacific University), Empire, Church, and *Missio Dei* (2011, at Southern Methodist University), The Wesleyan Tradition and World Religions (2012, at Trevecca Nazarene University), Holiness (2013, the joint meeting with The Society for Pentecostal Studies at Seattle Pacific University), and Atonement in the Wesleyan Tradition (2014, at Northwest Nazarene University).

Several of these themes show an obvious commitment to the established theological commitments of the academy and the church—Scripture, Holiness, Christology, and Atonement. Others reflect current and contextual issues—*Missio Dei*, Suffering, Friendship, the relationship between Christianity and World Religions—also featured in the discipline of academic theology seen in the American Academy of Religion, The Evangelical Theology Society, and the Society for Biblical Literature.

The dual concerns of the Society at these meetings were led by its presidents who organized and presided at the meetings during the decade--Craig Keen, Carl C. Campbell, Diane Leclerc, Thomas Jay Oord, Thomas Noble, Rob Wall, Elaine Heath, Michael Lodahl, Jason Vickers, and Richard Thompson. They each will be remembered along with the many other officers of the Society as leaders who remained committed to the WTS goal of combining the best of Wesleyan/Holiness scholarship and a vigorous witness to the modern world. They will also be remembered for leading the WTS in a decade that extended its boundaries to accommodate a wider and deeper fellowship of scholars committed to the work of the Society.

Chapter 8

The *Wesleyan Theological Journal*: A Brief History

by Barry L. Callen

Beginnings and Leaders

In 1980 the reports were favorable. For instance, Frank Baker, a prominent British Methodist scholar and professor emeritus of church history at Duke University Divinity School observed this: "One sight of the theological ferment of these last twenty years is the presence since 1966 of the *Wesleyan Theological Journal*, which has published more than a hundred studies of various aspects of Wesley's theology, especially as that theology was focused on the work of the Holy Spirit in human life."[1] The *WTJ* already had been on quite a journey by the time of that judgment in 1980.

The Wesleyan Theological Society, publisher of the journal, at first was the theological commission of the National Holiness Association, later called the Christian Holiness Association (Partnership). The WTS was born out of the concern and vision of a small group of NHA-related educators in various schools and denominations who sensed the need for a fellowship of scholars in the Wesleyan/Holiness tradition comparable to the Evangelical Theological Society.

Those first visionary leaders were Dr. William M. Arnett (Methodist), Asbury Theological Seminary, Dr. Leo G. Cox (Wesleyan Methodist), Marion College, Dr. Wilber T. Dayton (Wesleyan Methodist), Asbury Theological Seminary, Professor Merne Harris (Wesleyan Methodist), Vennard College, and Dr. W. Ralph Thompson (Free Methodist), Spring Arbor College. These men tested their idea with colleagues and found it feasible to begin serious planning.

---

[1] Frank Baker, "Unfolding John Wesley: A Survey of Twenty Years' Studies in Wesley's Thought," *Quarterly Review*, advance edition (Fall, 1980), 44-45.

A dream became a reality at the annual convention of the NHA/CHA in Detroit, Michigan, in April, 1965. Formed there was the Wesleyan Theological Society with Leo G. Cox elected the first president. At the first WTS annual meeting convened on the campus of Spring Arbor College in November, 1965, president Cox proposed in the business session the launching of an annual "bulletin." The WTS executive committee began work on a funding plan, and it was agreed that an editorial board would have the right to select, edit, and publish papers presented at the conference. The first issue appeared in the Spring of 1966. Professor Charles Carter, Wesleyan Methodist missionary educator, was the founding editor (1965-1972). The editors to date have been:

> Editors of the *Wesleyan Theological Journal*
>
> Charles W. Carter, 1965-1972
>
> Harvey J. S. Blaney, 1973
>
> W. T. Purkiser, 1974-1975
>
> Leon O. Hynson, 1976-1978
>
> Lee M. Haines, 1979-1981
>
> Alex R. G. Deasley, 1982-1986
>
> Paul M. Bassett, 1987-1992
>
> Barry L. Callen, 1993-2014
>
> Jason E. Vickers, 2015 to present

In addition to Charles Carter, the members of the inaugural Editorial Committee were Arthur M. Climenhaga (Brethren in Christ), Wilber T. Dayton (Wesleyan Methodist), and Armor D. Peisker (Pilgrim Holiness). Prominent leaders who also have served since as Editorial Committee members—in addition to the Editors—have been David Bundy, D. William Faupel, Stanley Ingersol, and Richard Thompson.

The contents of the first *WTJ* issue reflected the doctrinal distinctives of the new WTS organization. In that inaugural issue in 1966, Leo Cox wrote about "Sin in Believers," Kenneth Kinghorn about "Biblical Concepts of Sin," Kenneth E. Geiger about "The Biblical Basis for the Doctrine of Holiness," Wilber T. Dayton about "Entire Sanctification as Taught in the Book of Romans," while W. Ralph Thompson offered "An Appraisal of the Keswick and Wesleyan Contemporary Positions." These articles were intended to highlight distinctive features of the Wesleyan-Holiness tradition. They also began to lay the groundwork for significant debate soon to emerge in the Society.

Major Issues in the Early Years

The Nature of Scripture's Inspiration

The extended reflection on the nature of Scripture began during the business session at the first annual meeting of the Wesleyan Theological Society. It (1) addressed the integrating center and purpose of the Society—the scholarly consideration of the Wesleyan doctrine of Christian perfection, (2) impinged on the doctrinal statement of the Society and its developing articulation in the *WTJ*, and (3) helped to clarify and establish the nature of the relationship of the WTS to the National Holiness Association/Christian Holiness Association. The crucial question was the commitment to biblical "infallibility" as a condition for membership in the WTS.

The debate centered around the concept of "inerrancy." A statement found in the first issue of the *WTJ* said: "We believe that both Old and New Testaments constitute the divinely inspired Word of God, inerrant in the originals, and the final authority for life and truth." Prior to 1970 no official doctrinal statement was possible because the WTS did not have a constitution. But at the 1969 WTS annual conference at Marion College, a constitution was adopted in which the doctrinal affirmation of Scripture was revised to read: "We believe in the plenary dynamic and unique inspiration of the Bible...."

This revised statement first appeared in the *WTJ* in 1970 and continued appearing until the constitution was revised in 1978. This additional revision made its 1979 *WTJ* appearance as: "We believe in the plenary and unique inspiration of the Bible as the divine Word of God, the only infallible, sufficient, and authoritative rule of faith and practice." Later it was decided to eliminate any formal theological statement as a requirement for WTS membership, instead explaining that the WTS worked within the context of the CHA and its statement of faith/mission. This CHA statement included: "accept the inspiration and infallibility of sacred Scripture...."

Entire Sanctification and Pneumatological Language

Another issue soon was receiving significant WTS attention. In the 1972 WTS business session, George Turner of Asbury Theological Seminary suggested a panel on the subject of the Baptism with the Holy Spirit, with Reformed, Pentecostal, and Wesleyan representation and participation. The following year, Mildred Bangs Wynkoop reported to the WTS membership that the plan for the WTS doctrinal seminar at CHA would deal with the Holy Spirit in relation to sanctification.

This suggestion and plan likely were prompted in part by a provocative 1972 paper presented to the WTS by the Herbert McGonigle, a British Nazarene pastor-scholar, and printed in the *WTJ* in 1973. It raised the question of whether or not the use of pneumatological language in relation to entire sanctification can be found in John Wesley and early Methodism. There soon emerged a controversial atmosphere around this subject—see the *WTJ* issues of 1978 through 1980. In more recent years this subject has received renewed attention in the *WTJ*, especially with the writing of Laurence W. Wood and responses to them.

Moving well beyond these two early emphases, the journal has highlighted over the years a wide range of topics and hundreds of different authors. During the long editorship of Barry L. Callen alone, for example, 354 different authors were published. Callen and William C. Kostlevy released in 2001 a co-edited volume highlighting eight core themes found in the *WTJ* from 1966 to 2000 (*Heart of the Heritage*, Schmul Publishing). Each theme was overviewed and accompanied by a bibliography of published articles and the full reproduction of at least two from each core area. For instance, the first theme was the "Distinctive Wesleyan Perspective" and the reproduced articles were both by Randy L. Maddox—"Reading Wesley as a Theologian" (*WTJ*, spring 1995) and "Responsible Grace: The Systematic Perspective of Wesleyan Theology" (*WTJ*, fall 1984).

Focus and Format Changes

The Constitution and Bylaws of the Wesleyan Theological Society have for many years said this about the purposes of the Society: "A. To promote theological interchange among Wesleyan-Holiness scholars and other persons interested in this area; B. To stimulate scholarship among younger theologians and pastors; and C. To publish a Journal consisting of significant contributions to Wesleyan-Holiness scholarship." Embedded in these purpose statements are elements of continuing concern and sometimes changing practice. They are "and other persons," "younger theologians," and "pastors."

In 1975 the WTS responded to the call of some members to allow "outside speakers" at its annual meetings. It directed that guidelines be prepared for such a possibility, but with clear hesitation about any such presentations being given valuable space in the *WTJ*. The first guest from outside the tradition came as a panelist in 1984 at the annual meeting convened at Anderson University. He was John Howard Yoder, a Mennonite scholar fro the faculty of Notre Dame, who was asked to provide an Anabaptist perspective on the "primitivism" of John Wesley. His presentation did not appear in the *WTJ*.

The journal of the WTS was an annual production in its first years. There was consideration of it becoming a quarterly in cooperation with several related seminaries, but this never materialized. By 1978 a biennial plan was considered and became the case beginning with volume 14 in 1979. In 1978 the editorial committee was instructed to consider the inclusion of book reviews, research abstracts, and responses to paper presentations—a practice prompted in part by the intense exchanges of views in WTS annual meetings regarding the relationship between baptism with the Holy Spirit and the experience of entire sanctification. Book reviews became a standard feature of every issue.

In the most recent decades, two issues of the journal have been prepared and released annually. The spring issues have been oriented to the theme of the previous year's annual meeting of the Society, publishing select papers from that meeting, and nearly always including the address of the keynoter and the presidential address. Typically, the fall issues have been less theme oriented. They have included a range of materials received and selected without necessary reference to previous presentation to the Society.

In 2012 the Society authorized a significant change in the format and artwork of the journal. This was fully implemented with the fall 2012 issue, increasing the size and attractiveness of the publication, and also giving fresh attention to the professionalism of its production. Included was an increased formalizing of the role of the Book Editor and an enhancement of the peer-review dimension of article selections. With all of this change and as had been the case from the beginning in 1966, Old Paths Tract Society of Shoals, Indiana, remained the journal's printer and mailing agent.

Fresh Frontiers

In the early 1990s, the financial status of the WTS and *WTJ* was in serious difficulty. In 2015 that picture has been reversed dramatically. Up until 2009, large numbers of the back issues of the *WTJ* were maintained in hardcopy for distribution to new members, library requests, etc. Beginning in 2009 there has been available a regularly updated and fully searchable CD containing all of the materials of the *WTJ* from its beginning. In addition, digital files of each published article and book review are emailed to the respective authors and to non-members reviewers and requesting publishers. The journal is indexed in the *ATLA Religion Database* of the American Theological Library Association and is available in microform from University Microfilms International, Ann Arbor, Michigan.

The long *WTJ* editorship of Barry L. Callen (1993-2014) led to this comment in the last issue for which he took full responsibility (spring 2014): "After more than two decades as editor of this journal, I now am moving to new responsibilities. Serving you for these many years has been a great pleasure.... I leave with a definite touch of sadness, but also with a clear sense that the fertile world of Wesleyan scholarship remains rich and highly relevant to the needs of today's church and world." Indeed, may the fertile world of Wesleyan scholarship continue to flourish and be featured in the *WTJ*, a primary instrument of its scholarly communication.

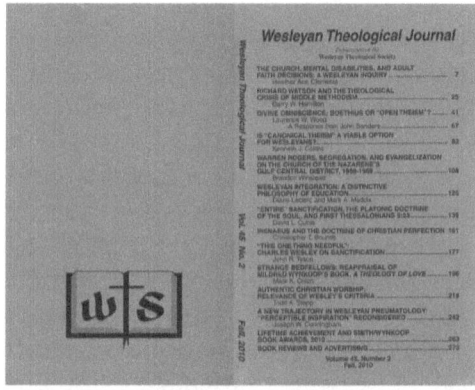

Chapter 9

Wisdom of the Presidents

by Barry L. Callen

Excerpts from select Presidential Addresses delivered to the Wesleyan Theological Society and then published in its journal.

John Wesley—Mentor or Guru?

Mildred Bangs Wynkoop (WTJ, 10, 1975)

At this, the tenth anniversary of the Wesleyan Theological Society, we must renew our own self-understanding. We are engaged in a big thing—how big we may not fully realize. It has not always been the "in thing" to be much concerned about John Wesley. One reason why it has become more intellectually respectable is that this age has found it necessary to reach for a solution to its massive problems, and it has found a possible aid in Wesley. Perhaps, by examining him and ourselves more carefully and honestly we may find the incentive to become bigger in ways that matter, in order to more adequately meet a day not greatly different from the day in which he served. Should John Wesley be our Mentor or Guru?

Martin Luther and John Calvin had a specific history-bound task to perform—that of defining their reforming movements before the somewhat hostile governments under which they existed. Wesley's task was quite different. What he did do was to unlock the scholastic doors to allow the vibrant "Word of God" to illuminate and vitalize the cold, correct Reformation theologies. The "man of one Book," as he called himself, added a dimension to theology that had never been an integral aspect of it before. The classic four marks of the church had fenced off the church into a sort of static, status-oriented, exclusivist entity. Wesley opened that closed door by showing that the church also has a mission. It exists to live Christian love in the world, to become, in Christ's stead, reconcilers. This changes the meaning of the church in ways that we are but slowly recognizing.

Our definitive label, Wesleyan, is both a mark of identification and an obligation to engage in self-criticism relative to the accuracy of the claim. This does not mean a slavish, wooden bondage to every detail of Wesley's very fluid and investigative and growing thought, but rather a full appreciation of the fact that his thinking was fluid, investigative, and growing and that he clearly distinguished between the substance (basic, biblical, and unchanging truth) and the circumstance (man's opinions about these truths and his appropriation of them) within theological conversation.

A mentor is a guide and critic. The task is to introduce his charge to sources of information, to prevent the student from drifting into unfruitful, erroneous byways, and to encourage him to exploit his own potential as he learns to master his field. A mentor is satisfied when his student outpaces him. By contrast, the guru is a master, a "prima donna" who is to be followed, obeyed, believed, imitated, honored. Innovation is not the prerogative of the follower. He sets aside personal initiative. So, which should it be? Wesleyans have used Wesley in both ways.

Wesley was deeply and consciously indebted to history, but history did not throttle him. He caught the torch from those before him and flung it out for others to carry. The flame has been spread far and wide: to Asbury, Roberts, Barclay, Albright, Morrison, Steele, Mahan, Inskip, Finney, Bresee, Rees, to name a few. The flame centers in the dynamics of "perfect love, not in history-bound scholasticisms which become the norms of Wesleyan orthodoxy. Wesley as mentor leads us into a biblical and vital concept of holiness. Holiness is the vitalizing spiritual energy which renews the churches through spiritually renewed people. The work of the Holy Spirit crosses all humanly divisive lines. When Wesleyanism is derived from Wesley as spiritual and theological mentor, it is possible to wear the designation "holiness" with grace, humility, truth, and winsomeness.

Open Theological Dialogue

Melvin E. Dieter (WTJ, 14:1, 1979)

We should note that we seem to be able to consider issues critical to the tradition with a new forthrightness attended by a spirit of mutual respect and love representative of the gospel we seek to proclaim. There is no other place within the structures of the Wesleyan-Holiness Movement which allows for such open theological dialogue among so representative a group of scholars. Our active participation provides a service which we can render to the Wesleyan-Arminian churches and people whose need for self-understanding requires definition and interpretation. But our Society must increasingly serve also as a means to explicating our relationships with other Christian traditions and the secular culture as well.

If Wesleyanism is to be more than an eddy in the backwater of religious life, much less in evangelicalism, an even greater willingness to face up to ourselves and to others than we have sometimes mustered is imperative. The viability of such debate, however, depends not only upon the dedication and integrity of this scholarly community, but also upon the willingness of the church community being served to allow the freedom to follow the search for truth in an atmosphere of mutual respect. This can be done out of our common concern for the integrity of the gospel and the mission of the church.

We cannot stand still; the experience of the people of God and the theological explication of that experience must go on--but always under the Spirit and the Word as the authoritative arbiters. In seeking any correction of deficiencies or mis-emphases in our theology or preaching, let us not fall under the apt description which was given by someone to theologians of the past generation: "In their rush to flee excesses they suddenly found out that they had left all their baggage behind." Let us be better stewards of our biblical, theological, and historical tradition than that.

Holiness and the "Protestant Principle"

Paul M. Bassett (WTJ, 18:1, 1983)

It is precisely the Wesleyan/Holiness Movement's doctrinal *raison d 'etre* that dictates that it be "Protestant." I refer to a quintessentially Protestant doctrine requiring a quintessentially Protestant context.

Negatively put, the "Protestant Principle" systematically forbids anything human the place of ultimacy in the church. No creed, no organizational structure, no person or group of persons, no custom or habit, no idea, nothing human is to be allowed supremacy. Positively put, the Protestant Principle systematically puts forward the absolute sovereignty of God, but not "mere" sovereignty. God's sovereignty is believed to be expressed in the gospel of Jesus Christ. It is God's sovereign will to redeem, and the gospel, as the expression of that will, comes to human beings where they are.

Protestantism also disavows the claim that it arose only, or even chiefly, as a protest movement. Rather, it sees itself as the fruition of long-developing "central tendencies" within the history of salvation. It sees reformation as an on-going, essential characteristic of the life of the church. This means that, while it takes the reformation of the sixteenth century to be critical to the history of salvation and paradigmatic as an expression of radical faith in the sovereignty of divine grace, it does not hold that particular reformation as normative or binding in all respects. Protestantism's commitment is to the sovereignty of divine grace, not to any particular expression of it or theological reflection upon it.

The Protestant doctrine of *sola scriptura* makes no idol of the Bible. This doctrine does not refer to the Bible essentially as a material entity, as a physical presence, although it is impossible to think of the Bible apart from these things. The basic point of reference is its ideational content. Only in Scripture do we have the divinely authorized account of who or what is really ultimate. Scripture is no ultimate as a written document, although it is the ultimate written document. It is the ultimate vehicle of truth, but it is not the ultimate truth itself.

Scripture is affirmed as authoritative for faith and practice because it is the sole reliable source (the church knows this by experience) of information and instruction concerning the one true God and what it means to believe in him. But even here the reliability of Scripture is understood not to lie in its mere words. Protestantism has insisted that Scripture becomes binding for faith and practice through the internal witness of the Holy Spirit, internal to believer and church. That witness is true and incumbent upon those who would be faithful. Scripture speaks savingly only as the Spirit enlivens it and witnesses to its truth. Apart from this witness of the Spirit, the Bible is only another religious book.

Here, then, is a theology that is thoroughly Protestant and faithful to the Protestant Principle. Ultimacy and supremacy belong to God alone. John Wesley insisted that the essence of Christian perfection is unconditional love to God and neighbor, an insistence that gives practical expression to the absolute sovereignty of God. Wesley resolutely and systematically puts down any pretenders to the throne: Scripture, reason, experience, tradition, good works, right worship, sound doctrine--the place of each of these is clearly outlined, both in their relationship to the divine sovereignty and in their relationship to each other.

It is precisely the doctrine of Christian perfection that provides the theological structure which maintains this negative side of the Protestant Principle. Pure love of God and neighbor allows none other on the throne but God Himself. Not even the doctrine of perfect love can take that place of ultimacy because perfect love is not an abstraction. It is more than doctrine. It is a grace-filled relationship and way of life.

Preferential Option for the Poor

Donald W. Dayton (WTJ, 26, 1991)

I have become increasingly convinced that one of the most important themes of contemporary theology is the growing claim that God's mercy contains an element of "divine partiality," and that this element is an integral dimension of the biblical witness which must find expression in the life of the church. To speak specifically, this claim is that God's impartiality and universal grace are qualified by a "preferential option for the poor."

It is "liberation theology" that has most forcibly brought this theme to our attention in the last couple of decades. But much earlier, this theme was a major part of the dynamic of the emergence of the holiness movement. It was the effort on the part of the founders of the various churches and institutions to maintain a vital contact with the masses in the face of the embourgeoisement of mainstream Methodism. It was explicitly acknowledged in the formation of the National Camp Meeting Association that a major motive was to cultivate the masses--the camp meeting was the vehicle designed for this purpose. This dynamic was nowhere more obvious than in the Salvation Army with its polemic against high steeple churches that neglected the poor and the masses. It also is seen in the battles over "free pews" within Methodism.

If indeed, a "preferential option for the poor" is a genuine feature of "scriptural Christianity," John Wesley's oft-quoted words of warning to the Methodists gain a new poignancy. He announced this in his sermon "Causes of the Inefficacy of Christianity":

> Does it not seem (and yet this cannot be) that Christianity, true Scriptural Christianity, has a tendency, in process of time; to undermine and destroy itself? For wherever true Christianity spreads, it must cause diligence and frugality, which, in the natural course of things, must beget riches! and riches naturally beget pride, love of this world and every tempex that is destructive of Christianity.

Integrating Heart and Mind

Don Thorsen (WTJ, 31:2, 1996)

My intention is to issue a cry of the heart on behalf of the intellectual life, a cry issued to those within the Wesleyan/Holiness traditions to become more attentive to that which Charles Wesley said so long ago in the words of a hymn: "Unite the pair so long disjoined, "Knowledge and vital Piety," learning and holiness combined.

Although our Wesleyan/Holiness traditions have not consistently affirmed the integration of heart and mind modeled by the Wesleys, we are poised to make more significant contributions to the intellectual well-being of evangelicalism and beyond if we support the historic and current trajectory of our Wesleyan/Holiness traditions toward a broadened and more active involvement in scholarship. It is my hope that there emerge a greater attention to scholarly reflection and output among academics, pastors, and laity within the Wesleyan/Holiness traditions. I do not, however, want that scholarship to be self-serving. That is, I do not want to promote scholarship just for the sake of promoting our academic and ecclesiastical institutions. Instead, it is my hope that scholarship produced by people within the Wesleyan/Holiness traditions will intertwine wonderfully with our already vital emphasis on spirituality and holiness. It is my further hope that the Wesleyan/Holiness traditions--along with evangelicalism as a whole--will have an increasing intellectual impact on contemporary American religion and society as a whole.

I am increasingly optimistic that this will happen. A primary example is the Wesleyan Theological Society. Established in 1965, it has grown significantly and now includes faculty, pastors, and active lay people. We have published the *Wesleyan Theological Journal* every year and now the bi-annual editions are longer and of increasing scholarly content. Our annual meetings have expanded to include outside speakers, concurrent sessions (patterned after the American

Academy of Religion and Society of Biblical Literature), and this year group discussions based on various disciplines (patterned after the Oxford Institute). Also this year, we have taken steps to establish an endowment for the Society and to change the annual meeting to the Spring, reflective of the growing scholarly interest among our members to attend the annual meetings of the American Academy of Religion and Society of Biblical Literature (AAR/SBL). WTS members have become progressively more involved in their professional affiliations. These are all signs of real hope for the future.

Life According to the *Telos* of Chrstian Perfection

Philip R. Meadows (WTJ, 41:1 2006)

My starting point is the conviction that John Wesley's theology presents us with a plausible intellectual vision and a compelling account of Christian life as *reality done differently*. His primary concern was not to provide us with metaphysical speculations about the nature of reality, or methodological considerations about how we can account for the truth of Christianity in a scientific and technological age. At his best, Wesley left us with the belief that real Christianity should be characterized by the idea of perfection, embodied in the means of grace, and extended through disciplined Christian fellowship.

Christian Perfection

Understanding Wesley's idea of perfection came to signify a whole way of being in the world, or taking up with reality, that encompasses every aspect of human life and experience before God. When Wesley is not being drawn into arguments about specific points of doctrine, he prefers to draw us into an exercise of the imagination where we can contemplate what daily life might be like if we fully embodied the scriptural accounts of real Christian discipleship. He presents us with an eschatological vision of reality done differently, and an invitation to take it up in the face of other "realities" that compete for our souls. Christian perfection should be thought of as a *telos* in the sense that it characterizes a whole way of life and salvation, and not merely the conclusion or consummation of it.

The Means of Grace

This *real* Christianity, characterized by the idea of perfection, is embodied in the means of grace. When considered as a whole way of being in the world, it is not surprising that Wesley includes both works of piety and works of mercy, and even the possibility that everything we do may be considered a means of grace in the broadest sense. This is because any practice can become a means of grace when it is situated in a way of life that takes up with reality according to the *telos* of Christian perfection. Indeed, anything else is but a formalism which takes the means as ends in themselves, or an enthusiasm that looks for ends without the necessary means.

For a church to take up with reality according to the *telos* of Christian perfection is to be on a journey in which we must learn to resist the machinery which silences the eloquence of real things and the commanding presence of God, while yet seeking to put all our ingenuity to the service of Christ. The mission of the church may well be an extended invitation to the world to join in this profoundly engaging journey with us, to do reality differently.

Conservative, Evangelical, and Catholic

Thomas A. Noble (WTJ, 46:1, 2011)

What are the essential characteristics that will help us identify the continuity and integrity of the Wesleyan tradition? They are that our theology is to be *catholic, evangelical*, and *conservative*.

Conservative

If this word implies being loyal to the Christian gospel, committed to specifically Christian, Christ-centered theology, refusing to dilute or syncretize the Christian faith, or to reshape it according to some alien metaphysic or according to fashionable modernity or postmodernity, then it is surely the case that Wesleyans cannot with integrity be anything other than conservative.

Catholic

We no doubt can all quote John Wesley's sermon on "The Catholic Spirit," but we have now buried the myth that Wesley considered all theological convictions as mere opinions and that he was ready to extend the right hand of fellowship to any and every heretic. Nor do we any longer need to say that by *catholic* we do not mean Roman Catholic--John Wesley included that tradition in the designation *catholic*. What we mean by the *catholic* faith is that faith *kath holou*, according to the whole, that faith which C. S. Lewis designated "mere Christianity" or which N. T. Wright calls "simply Christian."

Evangelical

It is surely somewhat contradictory to call ourselves Wesleyan but deny that we are Evangelicals. By this latter term we do not mean "fundamentalist" or "Calvinist." This is where the Wesleyan voice needs to be heard. We need to demonstrate that John Wesley, the "conjunctive" thinker, the one who produced a synthesis of the *evangelical* theology of the Reformation and the ancient *catholic* spirituality of Christian perfection, is a pivotal figure for today's global church. Only then will we demonstrate that the Wesleyan doctrine of "perfect love" is not the mad theological aunt in the basement of Wesley's theology nor a hobby-horse ridden by sectarians from the backwoods of American revivalism, but is the *catholic* doctrine of Clement and of Athanasius, of the Cappadocians and of Benedict, of Bernard and of Thomas. Only then will we prevent authentic *evangelical* faith from being "cabin'd, cribb'd, confin'd" in the exclusivism and rationalism of post-Reformation scholastic Calvinism.

The challenge to Wesleyan theologians is to think and write creatively in order to formulate this conservative, catholic, and evangelical faith in a way that serves the global, multi-cultural church of today. If we can serve the present age in this way, this is not the end. It is only the beginning of the service of the Wesleyan theological tradition. Thanks be to God!

No Holiness But "Social Holiness"

Michael Lodahl (WTJ, 49:1, 2014)

Holiness happens in the huddling of disciples around the locus of divine revelation. For Matthew, it is a gathering "in my name" that is assured of the very presence of the living Jesus Christ; for the Mishnah, it is a gathering "for the sake of Torah" that is assured of the *Shekhinah*, the very presence of God; for Muhammad, it is a gathering to hear the faithful and proper recitation of the Qur'an that is assured of the *Sakina*, the gift of divine calm, divine peace--and perhaps even of divine presence. What shall we make of these things, we members of the Wesleyan Theological Society? I have three suggestions.

1. However narrowly or broadly we might construe "holiness," if "holiness happens" when God "shows up" in the midst of creaturely realities, then perhaps Wesley has put us, his inheritors and successors, on a good path by insisting that "there is no holiness but social holiness." Admittedly, Wesley had in mind only the social phenomenon we call "the church," a relatively narrow construal of holiness. Our present ruminations are intended not at all to deny this Christian conviction, but to ask whether we can legitimately restrict social holiness to the church alone. We are asking here about the synagogue and the mosque, even as we acknowledge the morass of difficulties that such a question may well create.

2. Though Wesley did in fact have only the church in mind when he stipulated "no holiness but social," his liberating vision of divine grace opens up other possibilities. Think for just a moment about his sermon "Free Grace" in which he proclaims that divine grace "is free in all to whom it is given" and "does not depend on any power or merit in man," for all such human goodness or virtue "flow[s] from the free grace of God. Is it possible that the *Shekhinah* is indeed that "social grace" present and active within the Jewish community's wrestling with its texts over these many centuries, and thus profoundly a Torah-shaped Presence? Perhaps the greater challenge: Is it also possible that the *Sakina* is indeed that "social grace" present and active within the Muslim *umma*'s recitation, hearing, and obeying of the Qur'an over these many centuries, and thus a Qur'an-shaped Presence?

3. Finally, if these possibilities seem insufficiently faithful to the proclamation of Jesus Christ as "Emmanuel, God with us," hopefully we can follow Wesley as our guide at least as far as his sermon "On Faith" would lead us. In it he suggests a healthy agnosticism insofar as "it is not so easy to pass any judgment concerning the faith of our modern Jews." Indeed, admits Wesley, "it is not our part to pass sentence upon them, but to leave them to their own Master." As to Islam, Wesley in this same sermon dropped some intriguing hints about the possibilities of grace; he acknowledged that some Muslims were "being taught of God, by His inward voice, all the essentials of true religion."

4. Holiness happens, and it appears to be the case that "there is no holiness but social holiness." We might be inclined to argue long and hard against the notion that holiness happens in communal traditions other than the church. Or we might feel ourselves more generously inclined toward the synagogue but much less certain about the mosque. I am not trying to settle the issue; I am only trying to raise it. Denying the divine presence to synagogue and mosque does not automatically guarantee divine presence to us. If indeed "there is no holiness but social holiness," then finally the social onus is on us.

Diane Leclerc and Paul Bassett

Carl Campbell

Chapter 10

Recent Greats of the Tradition: The WTS "Lifetime Achievement" Awards

by Barry L. Callen

It is very appropriate to celebrate when celebration is deserved, to grant honor where honor is due. Accordingly, the Wesleyan Theological Society since 1994 has annually been granting its *Lifetime Achievement Award*. Those rare individuals have been identified who, over a lifetime of distinguished service within and on behalf of the Wesleyan theological tradition, have made outstanding contributions to its thought, life, and influence in the broader Christian family. Following are their names, photographs, the tributes delivered in their honor at annual meetings of the WTS. In a few cases there also are the responding comments of the honorees. These individuals and the tributes to them provide great perspective on the frontiers of the Wesleyan-Holiness tradition in the most recent generations.

> *Editor's Note*: The tributes and responses found below were published in the *Wesleyan Theological Journal* and are abbreviated. Not available are tributes to Charles Edwin Jones (2003) and Richard S. Taylor (2005). No award was given in 2006. All others are presented in chronological order of the years the award was received.

ROBERT A. TRAINA

The tribute by David R. Bauer, November, 1994.

Dr. Traina has devoted his entire professional life and remarkable gifts to the teaching of the Bible in the Wesleyan spirit. He was born in 1921 in Chicago, the son of Italian immigrants. His father was a member of the Methodist Episcopal Church, but served as a lay pastor at the Italian Mission Free Methodist Church in Melrose Park, Illinois. In this church Dr. Traina was nurtured in the Christian faith and first sensed the call to ministry at the age of sixteen. He majored in religious studies at Spring Arbor and Seattle Pacific Colleges.

While a student at Seattle Pacific, he became aware of the programs of the Biblical Seminary in New York and matriculated there in 1943.

The Biblical Seminary in New York, founded in 1900 by the Yale-educated Wilbert Webster White, had gained a worldwide reputation for the "inductive method" of the study of the English Bible, a hermeneutical approach that focuses on the literary analysis of the text. The goal was to allow the text to speak on its own terms, challenging all presuppositions and conforming the whole person to its message. Dr. Traina found this approach to be a liberating experience. He had come to seminary, according to his own account, with a deductive personality, and the inductive approach changed his orientation to life and the Bible.

Traina was appointed a faculty member by the Biblical Seminary upon his graduation. There he developed further the inductive method and its practical application, combining its traditional insights with the tools of traditional exegesis and setting forth the result in his book *Methodical Bible Study* (1952), universally recognized as the standard text on the inductive approach. No one in the Wesleyan movement has done more rigorous thinking about biblical hermeneutics or exercised more influence on the way the church thinks about interpretive methodology than has Dr. Traina.

In 1966, having earned his Ph.D. from Drew University, Dr. Traina accepted an invitation to join the faculty of Asbury Theological Seminary as Professor of English Bible. The next year President Frank Bateman Stanger asked him to assume the role of academic dean and vice president for academic administration, an office he held from 1967 to 1975, when he resumed full-time teaching in English Bible, retiring in 1988. As academic dean of the largest institution of theological education in evangelical Wesleyanism, Dr. Traina did more than any other one person to shape the educational philosophy and curricular goals during what were Asbury's most formative years.

He was theologically oriented. For him, the Bible is the ultimate source of the church's theology and life. The question always was: What is the theological significance of this passage? What role does it play in the whole of biblical revelation? How does it confirm, clarify, or in some cases correct what Wesleyans have traditionally held? Finally, he exemplified the biblical message, including the biblical doctrine of Christian perfection, in his own life and in his relationship with students. He was utterly committed to their welfare and their learning. In honoring Robert Traina, the WTS also recognizes the contributions of all those who teach the Bible from the Wesleyan perspective, who instill in their students the same enthusiastic commitment to the study of the Scriptures that John Wesley had.

THE TRAINA RESPONSE

In response to receiving this WTS award, Traina shred several deep concerns about what may be "a growing chasm between (1) our affirmation that Scripture and the God and Christ of Scripture are the supreme authority for faith and practice and (2) what we actually do in our theologizing and in our conduct." His concerns were:

> 1. One of the main reasons for the apparent growing dichotomy is the failure to test our faith and practice constantly by reference to specific biblical texts, interpreted properly in their grammatical, historical, literary, and canonical contexts. This failure obviously includes the use of "proof-texting," whose dangers we all recognize. But even more important and more subtle is the tendency to think of Scripture in terms of broad motifs, such as the Trinity, Creation, and Incarnation, and then to fill in the details, not by a careful and proper examination of specific biblical texts, but rather by using data which come from theologians and theological systems, philosophy, the behavioral sciences, experience, and other sources. In such a case, tradition, reason, and experience tend to shape biblical motifs instead of the specific data of Scripture shaping them. This is not to say that these extra-biblical data are not important; rather it is to emphasize the danger of using them in such a way as to distort what are purported to be motifs grounded in biblical authority.

> 2. We need to take the discipline of biblical theology more seriously, especially as regards what Brevard Childs describes as the ultimate task of biblical theology, namely, determining the relationship between the two testaments. The beginning point of doing biblical theology is what Gerhardus Vos calls "exegetical theology," that is, deriving theology from specific biblical texts, which harkens back to the first concern. The integration of these findings provides the basis for a biblical theology, including an understanding of biblical ethics. We are then ready to move to a biblically-based systematic theology.

> 3. The key to doing sound exegetical, biblical, and systematic theology is the proper use of inductive, inferential reasoning in contrast to a deductive approach, which may often be disguised as induction. True induction emphasizes the primacy and priority of a direct, firsthand approach to the biblical text itself, with a view to allowing it to speak its own message and attempting to determine the meaning and intention of its writers.

> 4. Interpretation should be an attempt to arrive at past-historical meanings and should precede evaluation. Much of what goes awry in biblical studies results from approaching the Scriptures initially with presuppositions that include value judgments. Such is the case with Bultmann's assumption that the universe is a closed continuum which makes miracles impossible. He therefore interprets miracle stories as "myths" that need to be "demythologized." Why not begin with the implied writer's point of view, that is, that God can and does perform miracles, and then attempt to discover what

the writer's original intention and meaning were in including miracle ries? Then, and only then, is one in a position to evaluate the writer's point of view, and to respond either in acceptance or rejection, that is, to decide whether to join the community of faith which by God's grace produced Scripture.

5. The approach to Scripture should allow it to speak for itself as literature. The Bible consists of a collection of literary units and should be approached as literature. Indeed, it can and should be approached like any literature. There is no need for a special hermeneutic, or for making a faith-commitment before interpreting Scripture. A general hermeneutic will suffice, without prejudice or favor. Such an approach focuses on the final form of the canonical text.

6. The church will not become biblically literate and thus be able to live and minister under the supreme authority of Scripture without a major emphasis on teaching the Bible to its members. The best kind of preaching, which in my mind is expository preaching, will not suffice. Neither will the kind of "Bible teaching" which is monological and which amounts to another sermon, often in the form of a homily. The kind of teaching I have in mind is dialogical and interactive. It is participatory in the fullest sense of the word.

Such teaching cannot take place unless the participants are taught how to examine the text for themselves. Direct Bible study is not only informative; it is powerful and dynamic and life-transforming. The Scriptures have their fullest effect when no intermediary stands between the text and its reader. Experts have a very important role in the study and teaching of the Bible, but we must not reserve Bible study for the experts. The Scriptures originally were addressed to ordinary readers, not to experts. They should be studied by all in order to realize their salvific and normative purpose.

JAMES EARL MASSEY

The tribute by Barry L. Callen, November, 1995.

I present to you a man who has been a personal friend and mentor of mine for decades. More importantly, he has played the roles of teacher, pioneer, model, and prophetic spokesperson for the whole holiness tradition in North America. This has been done from the pulpit, in the classroom, on the printed page, and in the streets with colleagues of his such as Martin Luther King, Jr.

James Earl Massey has embodied within the Christian community at large what his church of origin, the Church of God movement (Anderson), has envisioned since 1880 to be God's will for the church. The quest has been for true holiness and an authentic unity of the Spirit among all Christians. The vision has been one of changed lives that then become effective communicators and models of the gospel of Christ to the world. Massey has shown us how to be bridge-builders among all of God's people for the sake of the credibility of the church as it is on mission for Jesus Christ.

Born in 1930, native of Detroit, Michigan, son and grandson of ministers, accomplished concert pianist, acclaimed pulpit master, James Earl Massey holds degrees from Detroit Bible College, Oberlin Graduate School of Theology, and Asbury Theological Seminary—where he has a long tenure as a distinguished trustee. He was senior minister of the Metropolitan Church of God in Detroit for more than two decades. Serving on the Anderson University campus for most of the years from 1969 until his retirement this year, he has been Campus Pastor, Professor of New Testament and Preaching, and Dean of the School of Theology.

Beyond the Anderson campus, he was Principal of a School of Theology in Jamaica, radio speaker for the Church of God on its national program, the Christian Brotherhood Hour, and Dean of the Chapel and University Professor of Religion at Tuskegee University. He has been visiting professor, academic lecturer, or guest preacher at over one hundred colleges, universities, and seminaries. He is or has been a contributing editor for various journals, including *Christianity Today*, and was the homiletics editor for the *New Interpreters Bible*. Massey authored several bestselling books of his own in the fields of preaching and New Testament, including *Spiritual Disciplines*, *Designing the Sermon*, *The Burdensome Joy of Preaching*, and *African-Americans and the Church of God (Anderson): Aspects of a Social History*. This latter volume received the 2006 Smith-Wynkoop Book Award from the Wesleyan Theological Society.

Massey has filled distinguished pulpits from England and Egypt to Australia and Japan. A man of many campuses and of the whole church, he always has considered the Church of God (Anderson) in particular and the American holiness movement in general his home tradition. He has crossed racial and denominational lines freely, bringing with him the richness of the African-American church tradition. He has intruded on the secure smugness of human prejudice with the sharp edge of the biblical word of salvation, equality, and liberation for all. A 1996 issue of the *Wesleyan Theological Journal* carries a major article by Massey on "Race Relations and the American Holiness Movement." As few others have been able to do, he has bridged the gulf between faith and learning, religious ideals and social realities, and the ancient biblical text and the task of contemporary preaching.

With gentle courage, our Brother Massey has broached the reluctant racial barriers in North American society and in the church. His has not been an angry call for reparations; his has been a focus on the God who calls for believers to be present agents of the new creation in Christ, courageous members of a reconciling church that, once united itself by God's grace, can bring healing to a broken world. He has taught, preached, and practiced the good news about a *holy* God and a *holy* life in the midst of real human needs and urgent social dilemmas. Prophetically confrontational without ever being angrily abrasive, he is one man of God who is making a lasting difference.

The name James Earl Massey is known and respected widely as one of the most gifted preachers of the last half of the twentieth century. He is referred to in many circles as the "Prince" or "Dean" of preachers. In 1995 Abingdon Press released a major hardback book on Christian preaching for the twenty-first century, published wholly in Massey's honor, edited by myself and authored by nineteen of the top professors and practitioners of preaching in the church today. Titled *Sharing Heaven's Music,* this book reflects a fact known so well by the line-up of its distinguished writers. James Earl, poet/pianist, expert exegete, our special holiness brother, has done much to share the inspirations and implications of the Word of God, enabling insight, new life, hope, heaven's music in the pulpit, in the soul, and in the streets.

One finds this in the introduction to *Sharing Heaven's Music*, a direct reflection of the musical and preaching gifts of Massey:

> The gospel itself has a cadence, rhythm, and joy that should be music to the world. Its non-Enlightenment dimensions of vision, imagination, and poetic approaches to grasping and sharing truth are especially relevant to postmodern sensibilities. Designing a Christian sermon is an inspired art form as much as it is a learned skill. Today's multicultural settings, usually discordant, can be transformed by the harmonizing gospel so that diversity becomes a rich melody that witnesses to the God who comes to make all things new and all disciples one (pp. 11-12).

To literally thousands of ministers and ministerial students in dozens of denominations over a span of decades, the cadence and courage of James Earl Massey have been heard and seen. He is a humble yet powerful man of God who has been model and mentor, an honored and well-heard mouthpiece of the divine.

MELVIN E. DIETER
The tribute by Paul M. Bassett, November, 1996.

Melvin E. Dieter has truly exemplified the modesty, humility, and inconspicuous piety that are "our thing" as a Wesleyan-Holiness spiritual and theological tradition. He has exemplified the servant leadership, scholarship, and Christian collegiality which is the Wesleyan Theological Society at its best.

In 1924 Harold and Laura Dieter of Cherryville, Pennsylvania, became parents and named their son Melvin Easterday. Just south of Cherryville lies the city of Allentown. There, in 1921, the International Holiness Church had founded Beulah Park Bible School. Less than two years into the school's existence, the denomination (already the product of a number of mergers) became the Pilgrim Holiness Church (1922). In 1932 the school called Harold Dieter, pastor at Cherryville and treasurer of the school, to be its president. Within a year, under Harold Dieter's leadership, Beulah Holiness Academy, Shacklefords, Va. (estab. 1908) and Greensboro (N. C.) Bible and Literary School (estab. 1903) merged with Beulah Park and the "new" institution was re-chartered as Allentown Bible Institute. So, since his eighth year, Melvin Dieter, the son of that young, new "first family" of a young, reorganized school in a constantly reorganizing denomination with a fairly new name, has lived and breathed Wesleyan/Holiness higher education in one way or another.

Young Dieter was educated in the Lehigh Valley schools, received an A.B. from Muhlenberg College, a Th.B. from Allentown Bible Institute, and an M.A. from Lehigh University. Later would come an S.T.M. from Temple University (1953) and then a Ph.D. from the same university (1973). His doctoral dissertation was published in 1980 as *The Holiness Revival of the Ninetenth Century*. In it, he more or less takes up the story where his good friend, Timothy Smith, had left it in *Revivalism and Social Reform* (1957). In that work, in the work he edited which is entitled *Five Views on Sanctification*, and in the volume *The Church* which he co-edited with Daniel Berg in Warner Press' "Wesleyan Perspectives" series, Dieter clearly demonstrates the kind of diplomacy which we earlier underscored. His is an ecumenical vision, held from a clearly Wesleyan/Holiness standpoint.

From 1946 to 1948 he taught and served as high school principal and assistant to the president of Allentown Bible Institute. In 1948 he was named acting president, then president of the Allentown school. He was all of 25 years of age. For the next half-decade Dieter labored to rework the Bible Institute into an adequately supported liberal arts college. By 1954 it had become Eastern Pilgrim College in name and substantially in fact. In 1965 Dieter laid down the presidency of Eastern Pilgrim College to go to Temple University to work on his Ph.D. Many would remember those gifts and graces of leadership that Dieter had shown. They would not long allow him to immerse himself singularly in studies. For instance, the Pilgrim Holiness Church needed Dieter as a major player as it moved ever closer to merger with the Wesleyan Methodist Church. After the uniting conference was a reality, he was elected General Secretary of the Department of Educational Institutions, a position he would hold for eight years. Mel's major tasks were to instill commitment to a common cause and vision, and to reduce the number of schools brought into the new denomination by the merging bodies.

This ability to appreciate positively without loss of identity served him well, and in some ways served as the base for his next assignments—teaching church history and serving as Provost at Asbury Theological Seminary. Clearly, Asbury was moving into a new era—a more ecumenical but still Wesleyan era. More than a few among the various constituencies feared that the changes would bury the school's traditional identity. Here Dieter served for almost two decades, a stabilizing and guiding spirit, and clearly a "holiness man," but never a bureaucrat. It is during his years at Asbury Seminary that Mel served also as an officer in the Wesleyan Theological Society (Vice-President in 1976-77, program committee chair for the 1977 Annual Meeting of the Society, held at Huntington (Indiana) College, and as President of the Society in 1977-78). The two years 1977-1978 were watershed years in the history of the Society.

The title for Dieter's WTS Presidential Address fit his own character and the occasion. It was simply "Musings." His musings "on the moment" insisted that the Society must be a principal arena for conversation on issues of concern. He was not about to ask it to conform to the canons of public relations or even to give the slightest opening to considerations of self-preservation. Indeed, he said, the Society must explicate the Wesleyan/Holiness tradition to other traditions and to secularism; and to do this, we must listen to and understand each other as well as listening to and understanding those outside our circle. Mel called for the Society's Journal to enlarge its mission along the lines he had suggested. He called for full and free expression at meetings of the Society.

WILLIAM M. GREATHOUSE

The tribute by Rob L. Staples, November, 1997.

My first encounter with this year's honoree was in a church in Paris, Tennessee. I was a young boy about age nine and the occasion was a gathering of persons from several Church of the Nazarene congregations. On the platform was an unusually tall and unusually slim young man aged nineteen who seemed to be in charge of something.

His name was Rev. Billy Greathouse. Today, almost six decades later, he at least is still one of the tallest men I ever have known!

Later, I encountered Greathouse again, this time in a classroom in Nashville, Tennessee. I was a sophomore at Trevecca Nazarene College and had registered for the course "Introduction to Theology." It was taught by that same tall young preacher I had seen a decade earlier. I was quickly captivated by the enthusiasm of this teacher and his love for the subject. We were not more than three weeks into that course when I knew that no other academic subject I could ever study would interest me the way Christian theology did.

During the ensuing three years, I took every course Professor Greathouse offered. It was he who first suggested to me that I might consider making the teaching of theology my life's vocation, which I eventually did after seminary, doctoral study, and a few years in the pastoral ministry. It is, therefore, a distinct honor and privilege to have been asked to give this tribute to my very first theological mentor.

William Marvin Greathouse was born in 1919 in Van Buren, Arkansas. When Billy was four years old the family, Methodists, moved back to their native city of Jackson, Tennessee. Billy was baptized as an infant and received the Eucharist at an early age in a Methodist congregation. However, his family affiliated in 1935 with a home mission congregation of the Church of the Nazarene in Jackson, Tennessee.

Greathouse completed the first phase of his college experiences at Lambuth College in 1941 before pastoring and earning another undergraduate degree from Trevecca Nazarene University in 1944. He entered Vanderbilt University Divinity School, receiving a masters degree in 1948. By 1955 he was college chaplain and Chair of the Division of Religion at Trevecca, assuming the presidency there in 1963. He helped assemble at Trevecca a talented faculty that shared his vision of recovering a more "catholic" Wesleyanism. These faculty members included Paul Bassett, H. Ray Dunning, and Mildred Wynkoop. Then in 1968 he began his eight-year presidency of Nazarene Theological Seminary—after which the Church of the Nazarene elected him to be a General Superintendent.

Meanwhile, he wrote vigorously, with an overarching concern being to guide his denomination in a rediscovery and redefinition of its Wesleyan heritage. His publications have included *The Fullness of the Spirit*, and *From the Apostles to Wesley: Christian Perfection in Historical Perspective*. He co-authored *Introduction to Christian Theology* and *Exploring Christian Holiness,* vol. 2, and has contributed chapters to several other books, including *The Word and the Doctrine, Exploring the Christian Faith,* and *The Second Coming: A Wesleyan Approach to the Doctrine of Last Things.* He also wrote the commentaries on Zechariah, Malachi, and Romans in the *Beacon Bible Commentary.*

DAVID A. SEAMANDS

The tribute by Stephen A. Seamands, March, 1998.

We pay tribute to David A. Seamands for being a reconciler, a bridge-builder between two members of the same Christian family, two sisters who unfortunately had a rather nasty falling out during the first decade of the twentieth century. We, the members of the Society for Pentecostal Studies and the Wesleyan Theological Society, are the children and grandchildren of those sisters.

David Seamands was born and spent much of his boyhood years in India, son of Methodist missionary parents. He graduated from Asbury College, Drew Theological Seminary, and the Hartford Seminary Foundation, serving with his wife Helen as United Methodist missionaries in India from 1946 until 1962. On his return to the United States, he assumed the pastorate of the United Methodist Church in Wilmore, Kentucky, where he would serve for twenty-two years. Retiring from the pastoral ministry in 1984, he taught pastoral care at Asbury Theological Seminary, also serving as Dean of the Chapel from 1988 to 1992.

In 1962, when my father became the pastor of the Methodist Church in Wilmore, the two church sisters were just beginning to speak to each other again. Many of their children were not particularly happy about the new conversation. They were still determined to build walls, not bridges. As a high school kid living in the parsonage, I sometimes watched my father take the heat for what he was doing. At the time I had no idea how courageous he was.

In February, 1966, he preached a sermon on a Sunday evening called "The Holy Spirit and the Healing of Our Damaged Emotions." What he said that night about "damaged emotions" and "the healing of memories" is now old hat. But it surely wasn't then. One of the eventual results was a Seamands book published in 1981 and called *Healing for Damaged Emotions*, which now has sold over a million copies and has been translated into seventeen languages. It took for my father to do some of the things he did. In 1972, as the charismatic movement was in full swing, my father self-published a little book based on some sermons he had preached called *Tongues: Psychic and Authentic*. Again, the middle way he sought to chart between charisphobia and charismania seems quite appropriate now, but it was quite radical then—at least in Wilmore, KY. Throughout the book he praised God for what was happening: "There is no question that this [the new charismatic movement] is the most significant religious movement in America today. Every Spirit-filled Christian can do nothing but praise God for this gracious outpouring and pray that it will save both the church and the nation." He extended cautions and warnings toward charismatics, and he chided his own Wesleyan-Holiness tradition this way:

> Do you know why we are having such a great interest in tongues in our particular evangelical circle? Because long ago we ceased being a real movement of the Holy Spirit and became rather a kind of mausoleum to preserve a particular doctrinal interpretation.... We have gone overboard on doctrinal correctness and intellectual accuracy and liturgical precision. We have so prescribed and proscribed the Holy Spirit and we are so sure of exactly how He does things and the exact standards and convictions a man must have if he is to be filled with the Spirit, that we've lost the creative power of the Holy Spirit from our midst.... So God has allowed the neo-Pentecostalists and the charismatics to come along in judgment upon us.

Throughout his ministry as pastor of the Wilmore United Methodist Church, my father sought to create a community where the Wesleyan-Holiness and Pentecostal streams could flow together. One time he preached a sermon titled "My Lover's Quarrel with the Charismatics" where he encouraged his charismatic friends to balance Word and Spirit, to learn to appreciate the natural as well as the supernatural, and to desire the fruit of the Spirit as much as they desired spiritual gifts.

Outside of the Wilmore context, Dad frequently ministered with well-known charismatics like the Roman Catholic, Francis MacNutt, and was a speaker at the newly formed Oral Roberts University and at Faith at Work meetings where the majority in attendance were charismatics. That brings us to this historic joint meeting of the Society for Pentecostal Studies and the Wesleyan Theological Society with its theme, "Purity and Power: Revisioning the Holiness and Pentecostal/Charismatic Movements for the Twenty-First Century." Because of insightful and courageous pioneer bridge-builders like David Seamands, we are finally able to have this meeting. The two sisters are doing more than just talking to each other or tolerating each other. They are beginning to enjoy each other's company and realize that they need each other, even as the church and world need their combined message of the Spirit-filled life.

J. KENNETH GRIDER

The tribute by Paul M. Bassett, November, 1999.

Born in 1921 in Madison, Illinois, J. Kenneth Grider would emerge as a prominent pastor and theologian of the Church of the Nazarene. He was educated at Olivet Nazarene College, Nazarene Theological Seminary, Drew University, then receiving a Ph.D. granted by Glasgow University in 1952. He taught at Pasadena College (1952-1953) and Nazarene Theological Seminary (1953-1992). Grider was an unabashed lover of theological speculation and debate. His legacy deeply touched two generations of pastors in the Church of the Nazarene.

His doctoral dissertation was on the problem of natural evil in the light of the Christian doctrine of the Incarnation, written under the supervision of J. G. Riddell. Grider's practical interests came through as he argued for what he called a "life-situation solution" to the problem of natural evil. In Scotland he also formally entered his teaching career as an instructor at Hurlet College, the predecessor to the present Nazarene Theological College at Manchester, England. The dissertation was actually finished in 1952 back in the United States where Grider had taken up a post as Assistant Professor of Theology at Pasadena College. But already the wheels were turning in Kansas City and by the autumn term of the 1953-54 school year, he was at Nazarene Theological Seminary where he was to remain for 38 years as a teacher of theology.

Theology, taught Grider, "wears overalls and has legs long enough to reach all the way to the ground." Christian theology should be daily-life-oriented reflection upon the Christian faith. That basic conviction has remained a constant through all of the construction and reconstruction that Grider underwent as a theologian. He was bought up a devout Roman Catholic in the Illinois suburbs of St. Louis, Missouri, and in the Ozark Hills of the Show-Me State. That was back when popes Benedict XV and Pius XI were carefully trying to help Roman Catholics get past a long period in which that church encouraged the rank and file to stick to personal and corporate pieties and leave theologizing and other religious thinking to duly certified experts.

Grider came by his commitment to "theology in overalls" quite honestly. As a freshman, and now a deeply committed Protestant, he helped Olivet College move eighty miles north from its fire-gutted old campus to the vacant campus of St. Viator College. His very Protestant college now had to fit into the fabric of a former very Catholic school and neighborhood. Here was a parable on his own character—a profoundly Protestant religious experience in a very Catholic frame of mind. At Olivet, he discovered Stephen Solomon White who knew the Holiness Movement exceptionally well. White had a knack for teaching "preacher boys," as he called them (even the women), to love the church and to love theology and theologizing, always with real life in mind.

Such loves would mark Grider's insistence that the vocational task of a theologian is to guide the church's rank and file to understand and articulate their faith—to understand it well enough to articulate it in both word and work. Ministers and laity alike are to know both whom and what they believe with as much sophistication as possible. For him, theology is no ark of the covenant as it were—some body of holy and arcane intellection surrounded by mystery and approachable only by duly anointed, trained and garbed high priests. Rather, theology is everyone's business, and every Christian's business is to seek to articulate good theology across all of the terrain of daily life, guided by learned teachers and pastors.

In his early years as a teacher at the Nazarene seminary, he was noted for his concern to cite written authorities for almost everything he said. By the early 1960s, however, he was beginning to unfold his own wings. By then, he had himself become published, and therefore an "authority." His first book, *Repentance unto Life*, appeared in 1964, and it was followed the next year by *Taller My Soul*, then in 1980 by *Entire Sanctification: The Distinctive Doctrine of Wesleyanism*. His later magnum opus would be the 1994 *A Wesleyan-Holiness Theology*. Grider was one of three editors of the *Beacon Dictionary of Theology*. This and all of his works bear the mark of concern to put "theology in overalls," to help us all to see that theology "has legs long enough to touch the ground." In addition, especially since the mid-1970s, he occasionally has taken on the role of guardian and defender of the faith and confronted quite directly and candidly what he calls in his systematic theology "touches of error." This has put him in the role of rainmaker at more than one parade.

DELBERT R. and SUSAN (SCHULTZ) ROSE

The tribute by William C. Kostlevy, November, 2000.

Susan A. (Schultz) Rose is a native of Mountain Lake, Minnesota, and a life-long member of the Christian and Missionary Alliance Church. She was educated at St. Paul Bible College, Nyack Missionary College, and John Fletcher College (B.A. 1940) and received an M.L.S. degree from the University of Illinois. She has served as a librarian at Bethany-Peniel College, now Southern Nazarene University, and as Director of Library Services at Asbury Theological Seminary (1949-1978). She was a charter member of the Wesleyan Theological Society.

During her tenure at Asbury, she was a leader in the American Theological Library Association, the Kentucky Library Association, and the Christian Library Association. In 1967 she was named the "Outstanding Special Librarian" by the Kentucky Library Association. Always deeply committed to missions, she spent a sabbatical organizing the library at Union Bible Seminary in India. At the fiftieth anniversary celebration of Asbury Theological Seminary in 1974, she was given the seminary's distinguished service award. That same year she was awarded an honorary Doctor of Letters degree from Houghton College.

At Asbury, Susan Schultz (Rose) established the first evangelical scholarly journal, the *Asbury Seminarian*, but played a key role in founding the Wesleyan Theological Society. She created a greatly enhanced theological library and later she planned the construction of the building to house her collection. By the time of her retirement, her dream had been fulfilled in a collection of over 111,000 volumes housed in a state-of-the-art library facility, B. L. Fisher Library. In addition, her ministry lives through the lives of her protegees who include Donald W. Dayton, D. William Faupel, and David Bundy. In the early 1970s, it was Susan Schultz (Rose) who insisted that these three young scholars write three bibliographic monographs on the Holiness, Pentecostal, and Keswick movements. In the course of this assignment, she changed not only the lives of these young scholars but the course of evangelical historiography.

Talk of the "death" of the holiness movement must seem all too familiar to Delbert R. Rose (b. 1912). After all, it was common knowledge in the 1940s when he began his Ph.D. studies at the University of Iowa that the holiness movement had ceased to be a vital force in American Christianity. Rose was a scholarly pioneer who attempted a detailed study of the thought of a late nineteenth and early twentieth-century holiness camp meeting preacher, Joseph H. Smith. Implicit in the proposal was the unthinkable thought that a holiness evangelist was actually a worthy subject of serious research.

As a member of the Evangelical Church and a native of one of America's most fertile holiness belts, the central region of lower Michigan, Rose realized that holiness Christianity was not the exclusive property of such small Wesleyan denominations as the Wesleyan Methodist Church and the Free Methodist Church, or even of larger bodies such as the Church of the Nazarene. So unusual was this perspective in the late 1940s that, in order to write his dissertation on Joseph H. Smith, he had to first write an 80-page introduction to the holiness movement to establish the merit of such a seemingly dubious venture. Nearly fifty years later, Rose's work remains one of the best introductions to holiness movement. By insisting that the story of Christian perfection in America was far more than an account of the origins of distinctly holiness churches, Rose rightly located the enduring center of holiness Christianity in Methodism. The republication of *Vital Holiness* by the Schmul Publishing Company will allow a new generation to familiarize themselves with this enduring classic.

Perhaps of even greater significance has been Rose's role in the location and preservation of archival materials that document the history of the holiness movement. As historian of the National Holiness Association, now the Christian Holiness Partnership, he tenaciously pursued the literary fragments that constituent this documentary heritage while carrying a full academic teaching load at Western Evangelical Seminary (1947-1952), Asbury Theological Seminary (1952-1974), and Wesley Biblical Seminary (1975-1985). Rose's interest in the holiness tradition has always been more than purely academic. In the tradition of his NHA heroes, he has served as a noted camp meeting and revival preacher. His biographical sketches of the giants of the holiness movement which appeared in the Asbury Theological Seminary *Herald* remain an especially rich source of biographical data on often neglected holiness movement figures.

Even as the Roses have made significant individual contributions to the Wesleyan tradition, they have continued to serve internationally with World Gospel Mission and they have helped in the revitalization of Vennard College.

DAVID L. McKENNA

The tribute by David Bundy, March, 2001.

Salvation and sanctification came in the aisles and at the altar of the Holiness Tabernacle down the road, on the edge of town, "on the wrong side of the tracks." David McKenna, born in May, 1929, in Detroit, Michigan, found his way to that altar. He achieved at the local school. His parents' dream was for their son to attend God's Bible

School in Cincinnati. An encounter with God in a Free Methodist congregation being visited on a return from inspecting God's Bible School made other options available, and David enrolled at Spring Arbor College. He was graduated with an Associate of Arts degree in 1949 and, with his wife Janet, they moved on. At age nineteen he was assigned to pastor the troubled Free Methodist Church in Vicksburg, Michigan. While there he studied at Central Michigan University and received his B.A. in 1951. He was ordained the following year in the Central Michigan Conference of the Free Methodist Church.

Asbury Theological Seminary was the next stop on McKenna's educational journey. He received the B.D. and began work at Spring Arbor College (1953-1960) as Instructor of Psychology, Dean, and eventually Principal of the High School Program. He began studies at the University of Michigan, receiving the M.A., and then in 1960 the Ph.D. in higher education. In 1959, he became Vice-President at Spring Arbor College. However, when the opportunity came to go to Ohio State University to work with his Michigan mentor, he accepted and the family moved to Columbus, Ohio. McKenna served as Assistant Professor and Coordinator for Higher Education (1960-1961). Then he was invited to be President of Spring Arbor College. This was not a career move for an aspiring faculty person at Ohio State, but it was a decision to be faithful to his church, his faith, and his school.

Spring Arbor College evolved under his leadership (1961-1968) into a four-year institution known for its creative programs and good fiscal management. Then another institution of the Free Methodist Church called. Times were tough in Seattle, a one-business city. When Boeing prospered, there was money; often there was not. A bad decade at Boeing had left Seattle Pacific College struggling. As a student there myself, I remember the day the short, intense man walked to the podium in chapel and announced that we would survive and that, in order to be a Christian voice in the culture, we would become a "university." This created lots of discussion, but McKenna had the drive, tenacity, and grace to lead Seattle Pacific into that vision of Christian higher education. Seattle Pacific is today a prosperous institution and much of the credit must be given to the McKenna leadership of the University (1968-1982) through tough times and hard decisions.

From Seattle, McKenna moved on to Kentucky. In Wilmore, he inherited Asbury Theological Seminary, an isolated institution living beyond its means and divided against itself. The demands of being faithful to a holiness ethos and theology had brought it to exhaustion. McKenna did not transform the institution overnight. Who could? But he began with intentionality. The holiness work ethic served him well. Funding of his vision for Asbury Theological Seminary as a "player" in the realm of theological scholarship and a creative force in theological education remained for years an elusive dream. He negotiated with people of means about endowing the future of the seminary. His tenacity and understanding of human nature, first nurtured in the Holiness Tabernacle, served the seminary well. When the money from the Beeson family arrived at Wilmore, it moved Asbury Theological Seminary into the elite of North American theological education.

When McKenna retired in 1994 from Asbury Seminary, he left his presidential papers to the archives, and went on serving the Free Methodist Church and was Chair of the Board of Trustees of Spring Arbor University. He had been vice-president of the World Methodist Council, consulting editor for *Christianity Today*, a national radio commentator, founding chair of the Christian College Consortium, and Secretary for the National Association of Independent Colleges and Universities. He also had authored astonishing list of publications and been active in civic affairs in Michigan, Ohio, Kentucky, and Washington. The life of David McKenna has been devoted to service in the churches and institutions of the Wesleyan/Holiness traditions and to the cities that harbor them and the affiliations that support them.

A. WINGROVE TAYLOR

The tribute by Melvin E. Dieter, March, 2002.

It is my privilege to speak not only for the Wesleyan Theological Society, but for the whole Wesleyan/Holiness community and many others in the larger Christian family as well. We are not unmindful of the disclaimers given by a venerable colleague on an earlier such occasion. We recognize that when we glory, as we do, in the excellence and integrity of heart and life with which our recipients have represented our tradition, we above all give glory to God who in His goodness has so generously graced them.

Alaric Wingrove Taylor was born in 1923 in Charlestown on the Caribbean island of Nevis. His parents, Richard and Irene Blyden Taylor, met at God's Bible School in Cincinnati, Ohio, and were commissioned by the Pilgrim Holiness Church to return to Nevis and pioneer mission stations there. Nevis and the neighboring island of Trinidad quickly became strong centers for the Wesleyan/Holiness witness in the Caribbean. Wingrove was named for R. Wingrove Ives, a missionary colleague of his parents. His older brother, Ira, is a Wesleyan pastor in Washington, D.C. Two sisters, Katherine, a retired New York City schoolteacher, and Marie, a New York City registered nurse, make up the rest of the Richard and Irene Taylor family.

After grade school and some high school in Nevis, our Taylor finished high school and completed the B.A. and Th.B. degrees at God's Bible School and College. Later, he completed an M.A. in Ministry at Indiana Wesleyan University (1981). He is the recipient of three honorary doctorates. He and his spouse, Dorine Harper Taylor, have four children. They are: Brainerd, the founding conductor of the National Delt Chorale of Montreal, Canada, a chamber choir dedicated to the creation and performance of Afrocentric music; Paula, librarian, at the Barbados Public Library; Phoebe, emergency room nurse at the St. Francis Hospital in Indianapolis, IN; and Marie Grace, a school teacher also of Indianapolis.

While pastoring at Port-of-Spain, Trinidad, Taylor was a regular delegate to the Caribbean Field Conferences of the Pilgrim Holiness Church. At the time of the Wesleyan Methodist/Pilgrim Holiness merger in 1968, he was giving general leadership to the Caribbean churches as President of the Caribbean Pilgrim College in Barbados. He became a forceful advocate for the indigenous concerns of the overseas churches throughout the merger process, especially in the reorientation of the relationships between the North American Conference and its mission agencies around the world. He was on the founding committee of the new Wesleyan World Fellowship, which provided for other national conferences to take equal status in fellowship with the home conference. He served for twenty years as the first General Superintendent of the first such newly organized conference (The Caribbean General Conference) and for two quadrenia as a representative to the Wesleyan World Fellowship and chair of its executive committee, concluding his services in 1994. Wesley Press published his book, *A Theology of Adornment*, in 1992.

Taylor's persistent ecumenical vision placed him in the middle of the efforts to rally and unify the diverse evangelical communities and agencies scattered across the Caribbean. From 1973-1989 he served as the founding President of the Caribbean Theological Association. He was equally active in organizing and giving pioneer presidential leadership to the Evangelical Association of Caribbean Churches. He has been a member of the executive committee of the Association from 1977 to the present. He has also been a governor of the Caribbean School of Theology, was co-chair of the Congress on the Evangelization of the Caribbean and chair of the Wycliffe Bible Translators, Caribbean, is a director of Light House Literature, and is a trustee of God's Bible School and College.

All who know Wingrove know that, like the Apostle Paul, by the mercy of God he became a bondservant of Jesus Christ and ministering brother to us all. Dr. Taylor, we honor you for your concerns for an educated and disciplined ministry, for your efforts to bring together the Christian churches of the Caribbean for more effective witness, and for your gift of communication which, combined with rhetorical skills honed to a fine edge by your English Caribbean heritage, have opened up ministry for you in more than forty countries and on six continents. Ever passionate for the Gospel, your uncompromising call to discipleship and to righteousness inspire us to thank God for you

CHARLES EDWIN JONES

No published tribute available, March, 2003.

H. RAY DUNNING

The tribute by Craig Keen, March, 2004.

Ray Dunning is a graduate of Trevecca Nazarene College (B.A., 1948), Nazarene Theological Seminary (B.D., 1951), and Vanderbilt University (M.A., 1952, Ph.D., 1969). He was president of the Wesleyan Theological Society, 1985-1986, and authored or co-authored over a dozen books and many more scholarly and popular articles ranging in subject matter from theological ethics, historical, doctrinal, biblical, and philosophical theology to biblical commentary, hermeneutics, preaching, and biography. He began teaching at Trevecca Nazarene College in 1964 and retired from there in 1995, starting as Professor of Philosophy and Bible and finishing as Professor of Theology and Philosophy.

I first met Ray Dunning in the winter of 1975. I was a 25-year-old seminary student in Kansas City. Ray had come to town on Nazarene business. He had made contact with a couple of my friends who had been his students at Trevecca Nazarene College. Ray had made a deep impression on them. They were both quite drawn to Ray's broad theological vision. They had learned from him what was largely absent from some other religion departments of the colleges of the Church of the Nazarene, namely, an appreciation for 20th-century theology. In those days it was in the theology of Paul Tillich.

I again met Dunning when I was flown to Nashville to interview for a job teaching philosophy at Trevecca Nazarene College. I got the position and grew to love the place—in large part because of the atmosphere created by Ray Dunning. He let me do anything I wanted. And it took grace for him to do so. I was 31 when I joined the department he chaired, a "young gun" looking to out-draw the seasoned gunfighter who was the sheriff of this town. He had every right to run me out of Dodge. But he didn't. He let me teach my courses, take occasional pot-shots at him—and he would just smile, say something mildly humorous, and quietly go about his work.

Do not get the impression, however, that Dunning was a pushover. He was not easily dissuaded from the theology he had worked so hard to construct. And he could be quite intimidating. Not a few of his students felt the sting of his sarcastic rejoinders to questions and comments that struck him as dissociated from the serious work of the course. His time was poured increasingly into writing projects—particularly the composition of *Grace, Faith, and Holiness*, his 1988 Wesleyan systematic theology—and into graduate seminars that were populated by older students. He dreamed and planned Trevecca's M.A. program in religion.

Despite his academic prowess and productivity, Dunning's focus was absolutely on the local church. He saw his books, articles, and graduate courses in particular to be ways by which he might serve struggling pastors. After all, he had been the part-time pastor of two churches while he was still in high school and was ordained an Elder in the Church of the Nazarene when he was twenty years old! For fourteen years he pastored full-time churches in Tennessee and Arkansas.

Dunning set out to construct a theology that is grounded in the real life of real people in real churches. There is a profoundly pragmatic and existential dimension to all that he has done: life is to take place in the *living* God, and that life is to be a *virtuous* life that is centered in the God in whom all well-being has its roots, in the God whom we approach through the Christ who is always to be our norm, in the God who comes alive in us through the work of God's own Spirit.

RICHARD S. TAYLOR

No published tribute available, March, 2005.

PAUL MERRITT BASSETT

The tribute by Stanley Ingersol, March, 2007.

How fitting that Paul Merritt Bassett be honored here at Olivet Nazarene University, his alma mater. His theological education began much earlier, however. It started in the Nazarene parsonages, churches, and camp meetings of Ohio. But he came to this campus eager to learn more. Here he met Pearl, a young woman with Mennonite roots who became his wife. Here, too, he became a student of Carl Bangs, then a young teacher who helped awaken his interest in the Christian church's history and theology. Carl became Paul's lifelong friend, and years later they were reunited in Kansas City, teaching at two seminaries representing different households in Methodism's extended family.

After Olivet, Bassett attended Duke University. There he earned his seminary and then doctoral degrees. He came under the guidance of Ray Petry, a reigning giant in the field of medieval church history. Bassett's doctoral dissertation on Isidore of Seville was striking evidence that he accepted with pride the label of "medievalist" with a specialization in the religious history of the Iberian peninsula. He imbibed the Duke spirit of "critical orthodoxy."

Bassett taught first at Trevecca Nazarene College, then at West Virginia University. In 1969 he became Professor of the History of European Christianity at Nazarene Theological Seminary, where he taught for thirty-five years. His essential spirit is that of a churchman with a Wesleyan vision rooted in the Great Tradition of the church. In his view, the contemporary Wesleyan is to be in conversation with the whole church. His many publications are rich evidence of this broad conversation at its best.

Take Bassett's unique passion and long standing interest in the history of Iberian Christianity. Wesley had only superficial acquaintance with such things. Not Bassett. His passion to track the history of Iberian Christianity has taken him to countless archives and libraries throughout Spain and Portugal and to thousands of records, published and unpublished. Such an absorbing interest was, in part, an antidote to the sectarian mentality into which the Church of the Nazarene—Paul's denomination—had sunk by the mid-20th century. But sectarianism was never an option for Bassett. He has always had a strong attachment to the church's catholicity. And there are rich veins in the Christian tradition that John Wesley ignored and that his disciples have ignored even more.

Bassett has worked out of the conviction that a true Wesleyan vision must be rooted and shaped by the church's Great Tradition. This is evident in a cursory sample of the hundreds of articles he has published that carry such titles as "Practicing Holiness in the Great Tradition," "Children at the Lord's Table," and "Finding the Real John

Wesley." This concern also is evident in his volume *Exploring Christian Holiness: The Historical Development* (co-authored with William Greathouse) and *Holiness Teaching: New Testament Times to Wesley*. In these he makes the critical point that, if we look for the specific language of the Wesleyan-holiness folks among the Christian writers of earlier centuries, we will not find our shibboleths repeated there. But, if we search the writings of the Christian centuries looking for the fundamental notion of entire devotement to God, there is abundant evidence of reflection on and the practice of Christian holiness.

Bassett is known for several core convictions: that the cause of Christian holiness suffers most when it is reduced merely to being the basis for a sect; that the Wesleyan holiness churches could serve the Church of Christ better if they maintained their disciplined ways but viewed themselves as religious orders within the Universal Church; and that the truth be told even when it is unpleasant. He has been visiting professor at Fuller Theological Seminary, Central Baptist Theological Seminary, the University of Kansas School of Religion, and the University of Missouri-Kansas City. His international teaching experience includes assignments in Spain, England, Mexico, Costa Rica, Australia, The Philippines, and several institutions in South America.

His involvements have been numerous. He has been a consulting editor to *Christianity Today*, a resident scholar of the Institute of Ecumenical and Cultural Research, and a member of the board of editors of the online *Journal of Southern Religion*. He has served the Wesleyan Theological Society in various capacities: in 1981-82 as its 18th president, from 1987 to 1993 as editor of the *Wesleyan Theological Journal*, and for many years as one of our ecumenical representatives to the Commission on Faith and Order.

ROB L. STAPLES

The tribute by K. Steve McCormick, March, 2008.

The German poet Goethe once said, *"What you have as heritage, Take now as task; for thus you will make it your own!"* Well, for over four decades, Dr. Staples worked faithfully at his task of serving the gospel of Christ within his own church tradition—the Church of the Nazarene—in preaching and shepherding, teaching and writing.

Rob Staples was born in 1929 and received his B.A. from Trevecca Nazarene College (1951), B.D. from Nazarene Theological Seminary (1954), and Th.D. from Pacific School of Religion (1963). He pastored in California before having an illustrious teaching ministry at Southern Nazarene University (1963-1976) and then Nazarene Theological Seminary (1976-1998). While working mostly in systematic theology, and more specifically in the life and thought of John Wesley, Staples has attempted to correct some of the missteps that the Holiness Movement has taken in appropriating Wesley's message so that the church will be faithful in her task of serving the Gospel. This has not been done without sacrifice. We all know that many of the great prophets and reformers of the church have been met with fierce opposition and suffering. Staples belongs to this company of the faithful.

The Staples' ministry of correction began with his doctoral dissertation titled "John Wesley's Doctrine of Christian Perfection: A Reinterpretation." Many within the Wesleyan Theological Society will recall how in the late 1970s and early 1980s the "baptism with the Holy Spirit" debate filled the pages of our Society's journal and took much time and reflection from our scholars. Staples responded with the faithful care and Noah-like wisdom by protecting the ark of the Wesleyan tradition in both the academy and the church. During this time he produced a paper that would become a watershed moment in the Church of the Nazarene's history. Unfortunately, the tradition of the church was not always ready to receive such a "corrective."

Because of his faithful service and wise counsel, countless students and ministers would be saved from slipping into destructive cynicism and leaving the Wesleyan tradition. Many of Staples' students can still hear the following paraphrase from one of his most memorable sermons on the church: "Noah listened patiently to his sons nagging complaints about the living conditions on the ark—can you imagine the smell and muck from all of those animals?—and quipped, 'go down below the deck and you will find all the tools you need to make whatever renovations you deem necessary, just don't put a hole in the ark and sink it, it's all we've got.' "

That is a living, breathing, smelling metaphor of the church that has kept many former students of Staples faithful to the task of the church! In many ways, his careful and courageous scholarship would eventually blaze a new trail within the holiness movement for the young and sometimes upstart scholars attempting to work faithfully at their own task of "correcting and fulfilling" their tradition. His service has taught us how to handle the "living faith of the dead."

Later on in his scholastic work, Staples would once again use his expertise and love of John Wesley to help correct the misunderstandings and aberrations regarding the place of the sacraments in a tradition. His 1991 book *Outward Sign and Inward Grace: The Place of Sacraments in Wesleyan Spirituality*, would not only receive high praise and recognition by someone like Martin Marty, but also would become a critical resource for numerous students and ministers seeking to make the holiness tradition their own, while reconnecting this tradition to the "one, holy, catholic and apostolic church." Showing his playful and well as insightful side, he also authored *The Church Out on a Limerick* (2000) and *Words of Faith* (2001).

The influence of Staples now reaches deep into this Society and the church at large. He has former students teaching in every Nazarene college, university, and seminary in the United States and in several other countries. Many of his students have been active in this Society, and some have gone on to serve as its president, including Diane Leclerc (our presiding president), Stephen Gunter, Randy Maddox, Steve McCormick, Craig Keen, and Tom Oord. Staples himself served as president in 1975-1976.

Rob Staples, we have heard you calling us in the very person of Christ to stand with you and all the company of heaven as we take our heritage in the body of Christ as our task and work to make it our own. We stand by you and honor you.

BARRY L. CALLEN

The tribute by Richard P. Thompson, March, 2009.

Born in 1941, in New Brighton, Pennsylvania, Barry L. Callen knew from his beginning the Wesleyan tradition of the Free Methodist Church. Family circumstances in the Ohio of his youth led him to become affiliated with the Church of God (Anderson) and to do his undergraduate studies at Geneva College back in Pennsylvania. His call to Christian ministry led him to attend seminary after college graduation in 1963. First it was the Master of Divinity at Anderson School of Theology, then the Master of Theology at Asbury Theological Seminary, and finally the Doctor of Religion at Chicago Theological Seminary, later adding a doctorate in higher education administration at Indiana University. These diverse settings would help enable Callen to make substantive contributions to the Church of God movement and the Wesleyan/Holiness movement at large.

Apparently, Anderson University saw something remarkable in this fledgling scholar. He would teach with distinction in both the undergraduate and graduate programs of the university. In 1988 he was named by the Board of Trustees as the first "University Professor," a special faculty rank to recognize a senior and distinguished scholar-teacher of the faculty. In addition to his teaching, his leadership of forty years in the Anderson academic community is evident in the wide variety of positions that he has held, including: department chair, founding director of the Center for Pastoral Studies, dean of the graduate School of Theology, dean of the undergraduate college, Vice President for Academic Affairs of the university, Secretary of the Board of Trustees, and founding Editor of Anderson University Press.

While carrying heavy responsibilities in teaching and administration, Callen managed to squeeze out hours here and there for writing, with the result that now he has authored or edited more than forty books, including *God As Loving Grace* (1996), *Radical Christianity* (1999), *Authentic Spirituality* (2001), *Discerning the Divine* (2004), *The Scripture Principle*, co-authored with Clark H. Pinnock (2006), a commentary on the New Testament book of Colossians (2007), a documentary history of his own fellowship, the Church of God (*Following the Light*, 2000), *Reading the Bible in Wesleyan Ways* (co-edited with Richard Thompson in 2004), and many more. In 1992 he published the history of Anderson University, *Guide of Soul and Mind*, and later in 2007 would come *Enriching Mind and Spirit* offering brief histories of all the higher education institutions of the Church of God. Three novels would follow, the first released in 2009.

Callen's monumental contribution, both to the Wesleyan Theological Society specifically and to the Wesleyan/Holiness movement generally, has come in his extended tenure as editor of the *Wesleyan Theological Journal* (1993-2014). When he first assumed the editorship, a tenuous financial situation threatened the future of the journal and of the Society itself. However, these difficulties are now found only in the difficult memories of those past years, with the journal's and the Society's rejuvenation due in no small part to Callen's consistent and tireless editorial leadership. Later he would also assume the editorship of the new Aldersgate Press of the Wesleyan Holiness Consortium.

There is one more side to this man that reveals something about his heart. In 2001, Dr. Callen with three others founded a Christian mission organization called Horizon International, which is now a significant player in assisting AIDS orphans in six countries of southern and eastern Africa. As John Wesley once insisted, and Callen so well reflects, there is no holiness that is not also social holiness!

THE CALLEN RESPONSE

Some 130 years ago, Daniel Warner, primary pioneer of the Church of God movement (Anderson), *walked out* of the holiness association in this state [Indiana], looking outside all church associations for the perfect church that God intends. His vision—holiness is the key to Christian unity, and thus effective Christian mission. His irony—we'll have to separate in order to get together! Well, although a loyal son of Warner's tradition, obviously I have chosen to *walk back in*.

Being among you across recent years, I have watched both the soul- searching and the witnessing of the Wesleyan, Holiness, and Pentecostal traditions. I've been very much at home. God indeed does want a sanctified, Spirit-filled, and unified people, and we'll have to stay *together* to help it be a reality. For the opportunity to be one of you, and to serve the great cause of Christ with you, I am in your debt.

Over my nearly three decades as your journal editor, I have worked at close range with your most creative writings. You have been my teachers, and I am much the better for it. My 2008 autobiography is titled *A Pilgrim's Progress*. There and elsewhere, I have observed that the larger Christian community is on a crucial journey. Reflecting the view of my own ecclesial community, the Church of God (Anderson), I believe that the continuing progress of this divinely-inspired journey will necessarily go through a holiness message, probed, retooled, proclaimed, and boldly lived by the church's best—many of whom are associated with the Wesleyan Theological Society.

Over the years I have watched at close range the Wesleyan, Holiness, and Pentecostal traditions give leadership to serious dialogues with scientists, philosophers, psychologists, historians, biblical scholars, educators, "open" theologians, "process" theologians, Eastern Orthodox patriarchs, and more. The depth, range, and unifying power of the tradition rooted in the Wesleys keeps being evidenced in all of these dialogues, and with many of you in the lead. To have been with you in the process of dialoging, probing, and publishing about this great tradition has been a personal privilege.

DONALD W. DAYTON

The tribute by Don Thorsen, March, 2010.

Scholars generally become great through their various accomplishments and publications. However, a few of them provide a paradigm shift in how we understand the world in which we live. Donald W. Dayton is a scholar who has dramatically changed the ways we view Christianity, theology, and ethics. He has impacted both church and academy, and Christian traditions both mainline and evangelical, Wesleyan and Pentecostal.

Donald Dayton was born in 1942, nurtured by the Wesleyan Church, and educated with a Bachelor of Arts from Houghton College, a Bachelor of Divinity from Yale Divinity School, a Master of Library Science from the University of Kentucky, and a doctorate in Christian theology from the Divinity School of the University of Chicago. He taught at Asbury Theological Seminary (1969-1972), North Park Theological Seminary (1972-1979), Northern Baptist Theological Seminary (1979-1997), Drew University (1997-2002), and Azusa Pacific University (2002-2004), retiring in 2004.

The scholarly accomplishments of Dayton are numerous. Early in life, he contributed to publication of the magazine *The Post-American*, later called *Sojourners,* and affiliated with Evangelicals for Social Responsibility. He was an original drafter and signer of "The Chicago Declaration of Evangelical Social Responsibility" (1973). Don has long manifested concern for the varieties of impoverishment from which people suffer, and advocated on their behalf. In addition to extensive writing, he served in several editorial capacities. A *Festschrift* published in his honor is 2007 is titled *From the Margins: A Celebration of the Theological Work of Donald W. Dayton*. Most prominent among his own works are *Discovering an Evangelical Heritage* (1976), *Theological Roots of Pentecostalism* (1991), and *The Variety of American Evangelicalism* (2001), edited with Robert K. Johnston. In *Discovering an Evangelical Heritage*, Don did groundbreaking historical work in promoting the social relevance of the Holiness heritage and how it served as an evangelical forerunner in the nineteenth century. *Theological Roots of Pentecostalism* is a landmark study of how Pentecostalism grew out of Methodism and nineteenth-century Holiness revivals.

Dayton became the only person to be elected president of both the Society for Pentecostal Studies (1988) and the Wesleyan Theological Society (1989), laying the groundwork for joint meetings between these two societies. He participated beginning in 1983 in work with the Commission on Faith and Order of the National Council of Churches, representing the Wesleyan Theological Society. In 2007 he delivered a plenary address at the 50th anniversary of Faith and Order at Oberlin College, outlining the importance of Oberlin for the Holiness heritage as well as for ecumenism. He expanded our understanding of the Wesleyan, Holiness, and Pentecostal traditions, and of evangelicalism more broadly conceived, of social consciousness and advocacy on behalf of the poor, and of the need for ecumenical dialog and cooperation.

THE DAYTON RESPONSE

This award is especially meaningful because I have spent my career in semi-exile from the Holiness Movement. Denied ordination by the Wesleyans over my inability to affirm the "inerrancy" of Scripture, I have spent only five of my thirty-five years on seminary faculties within the tradition, my first three at Asbury Theological Seminary and the last two here at Azusa Pacific University. This has actually proved to be creative, while requiring occasionally some fancy footwork. I have not been subject to ecclesiastical authority and thus able to follow my own path and give my rather contrarian personality freer reign. And this "exile" has made it easier to be more enthusiastic about the Holiness Movement since I have not had to live in proximity to its legalistic and often provincial ethos. From this distance I have even been able to appreciate that movements ethically fussy about drinking, card playing, and dancing have been sensitive to slavery, the oppression of women and the poor, etc. An illuminating but difficult discovery!

My interest in the Holiness Movement was either accidental or providential. Intellectually, like many of you on a trajectory toward greener theological pastures, I nonetheless rejected an offer from Princeton and instead went to Asbury Theological Seminary for my first job (comparable salary, but cheaper housing in Wilmore!). The American Theological Library Association held a meeting at Pasadena College (now Point Loma Nazarene University) and had a practice of inviting a bibliographic essay on the host tradition. My boss, Sue Schultz, couldn't convince the Christian Holiness Association official historian, Delbert Rose (much later her husband), to spend money on the trip. She turned to me and twisted my arm, relieving me of most of my library work for about half a year. I protested that I had never read any holiness literature and had no intention of doing so. She persisted; I yielded. I left Asbury with a single shelf of holiness literature that eventually grew to over 10,000 volumes--now housed at Fuller Theological Seminary.

This attraction to the Holiness Movement gained impetus when I discovered as book editor of *Sojourners* that the Wesleyan Church (in its early abolitionism, feminism, and pacifism) had been a close historical parallel to the position that we were developing under the influence of the civil rights and anti-Vietnam War movements. This resulted in the articles that became *Discovering an Evangelical Heritage*. The rest of my intellectual journey can be seen as a struggle with the puzzles of that book. Illustrating this is my increasing rejection of the reigning "evangelical" historiography that starts with fundamentalism and privileges something like the Orthodox Presbyterian Church as the paradigmatic "evangelical" church. I am convinced that we should turn this on its head and use the Holiness Movement to explain the two-party system of American Protestantism by privileging the Christian and Missionary Alliance and the themes of its "four-fold" gospel (Jesus as Savior, Sanctifier, Healer, and Coming King).

My work in the Wesleyan Theological Society has been a roller coaster ride. For many years the office of promotional secretary provided the leverage for change from the "margins." It is hard to imagine now that nearly four decades ago the very idea of "outside speakers" was so controversial that it could be considered only by a secret written ballot—and I then set the idea back several years by proposing Pentecostal scholar Vinson Synan who was already a member of our society. Some years ago my friend Billy Abraham chided me for my continuing involvement in such a reactionary society. I replied to the contrary that the society was at least a decade ahead of what I'd anticipated.

My involvement in the World Council of Churches and National Council of Churches has been an extension of my interest in the Holiness Movement and my efforts to create greater awareness of it in the larger church world. Far from a diluting experience, this has pushed me even closer to the Holiness Movement as I have articulated its larger significance. In this work, I have struggled with one of the most difficult issues facing the movement--whether to pursue a strategy of assimilation and reinsertion of the Holiness Movement into the classical tradition or to witness to its radical forms of witness against it. The sociological forces that we all carry favor the former. I have been increasingly drawn to the latter—not always an appreciated option, either here or there.

Finally, a word about Pentecostalism. My dissertation argued that Pentecostalism was born in the radical wing of the Holiness Movement, a thesis that flew in the face of the position of our great historian, Timothy Smith. Misunderstanding my intentions, he and the Christian Holiness Association leadership fought my work viciously, while I found more receptivity in the Society for Pentecostal Studies. My motion in our Oklahoma City meeting to send greetings upon the founding of SPS was seconded only so that it could be debated and the minutes expunged of any reference to it. I was later deeply moved when the SPS changed its constitution to invite me to be president. I accepted, assuming this would end my career in WTS. I was astounded to be immediately elected the president of WTS, so that for one week I served at the head of both societies. I planned a WTS program adjunct session that explored the historical relationship between the movements. Now we meet together every five years. This work may well have been my most important ecumenical achievement.

HOWARD A. SNYDER

No published tribute. Dr. Snyder's Response, March, 2011.

Recently I have been reading Veli-Matti Kärkkäinen's book *The Trinity: Global Perspectives*. In discussing Asian views of the Trinity, Kärkkäinen notes that a sharp criticism of Western theology raised by some Asian theologians is the Western tendency to think in either/or categories. To quote Kärkkäinen, summarizing the Eastern criticism: "Western thinking is founded on the dualistic principle of the excluded middle. A sentence can be only true or false, not both-and. The Asian way of thinking resists that kind of either/or distinction" (313). Kärkkäinen cites in particular the criticisms voiced by theologians Raimundo Pannikar and Jung Young Lee.

We may debate whether the criticism is valid or not. At the least, it certainly needs some qualification. However, I think we can acknowledge some truth here. Western theology often does tend to either/or ways of thinking that fail to grasp the breadth and depth of the biblical gospel, and this is particularly true of highly rationalistic forms of theology, including much of Evangelicalism.

To me, one of the great strengths of John Wesley's thought and practice is precisely its inclusive, both-and character. We could list many examples—"all inward *and* outward holiness," "justice, mercy, *and* truth," "holiness *and* happiness." Or, more fundamentally, there is Wesley's affirmation of *both* God's sovereignty and human freedom, of *both* salvation by faith and the necessity of good works, and the continuing value of the law despite the priority of grace. There also is his insistence that salvation is *both* a present and an eschatological reality—or, more accurately, that it is present as fact, promise, and process, all at once, and it is future according to the sure promise of the full "restoration of all things."

I noted this conjunctive feature of Wesley's theology in a chapter called "The Wesleyan Synthesis" in my 1980 book, *The Radical Wesley*. And as I comment in my new book *Yes in Christ: Wesleyan Reflections on Gospel, Mission, and Culture* (16-17):

> Wesley had several unusual advantages that lifted his vision beyond that of most figures in Christian history. He was blessed with a well-informed Christian upbringing, especially with a wise mother who helped him think deeply. He had a both/and rather than an either/or mind, both rational and poetic, fascinated by language, alert to metaphor and paradox, yet interested in logic and in scientific discovery (both right-brained and left-brained, we would say today). He was a voracious reader with broad and eclectic tastes. His grounding in the Anglican *via media* of Scripture, reason, and tradition gave him historical and theological breadth. He studied at Oxford during the rediscovery of early Christian sources.

Further, Wesley lived at the height at the Age of Reason but also at the beginning of new interest in human experience and emotion or "enthusiasm." He read of the discoveries coming from the "New World" and England's far-flung empire. He experienced the Industrial Revolution and experimented with the newly-discovered force of electricity. In short, he inhabited "the Age of Wonder" when "the Romantic generation discovered the beauty and terror of science," as historian Richard Holmes puts it.

The conjunctive nature of Wesley's theology runs deep. Some of my doctoral students from Asia have picked up on this and explored its theological and missiological implications for their contexts. The more we understand the deep inclusive structure of Wesley's theology, the more we find it necessary to make a clear distinction between *John Wesley's* theology and *Wesleyan* theology. Wesleyan theology, of course, runs into many streams and eddies. A general critique I would make is that most versions and streams of Wesleyan theology accent certain themes in Wesley and tend to ignore others—a common phenomenon in the theological followers of any creative leader in history. This one-sided tendency in dealing with Wesley started during his lifetime, as we know, and has continued as theologians in the generations immediately following Wesley tried to force his teachings into the categories of systematic theology. This one-sidedness continues up to the present.

One of the starkest examples was the bifurcation in Wesleyan theology in the nineteenth century as seen in the Holiness Movement, on the one hand, and attempts to recast Wesley's theology in the forms of rising European liberalism and rationalism, on the other. Today, of course, theologians want to recast Wesley in terms of process theology, "open theism," liberation theology, discourse analysis, or a reaffirmation of systematics. So it goes. Thus, I see the vital necessity of studying Wesley *on his own terms* and *within his own context.* Equally important is the necessity to keep our theology carefully grounded in Scripture, as Wesley was concerned above all to do.

I discovered this both/and, conjunctive character of Wesley's theology only when I began reading Wesley systematically in seminary and in the years following. The fundamental insight is that truth is found not in either/or discursive, linear thinking but in an appreciation of paradox and bridging perspectives. This insight initially came to me, however, not from reading Wesley but from the sermons of the remarkable nineteenth-century Anglican preacher, Frederick W. Robertson (1816-53). Robertson made the point that often truth is found not in one side or the other of an argument, nor simply in a "golden mean" or midpoint between, but in acknowledging the degree of truth that may exist in opposing viewpoints and discerning how to synthesize them coherently and experientially (not just conceptually). I helpfully encountered Robertson during a "great preachers" course at Asbury Theological Seminary with a visiting professor from England, Dr. Bishop. This way of thinking avoids both extremes, (1) overly-categorical rationalism and (2) a non-rational or irrational affirmation of paradox or mystery.

This is simply the recognition that God's truth, and thus the truth of nature, history, and human experience, is so grand that it readily transcends our rational tools and categories. Still, it is fundamentally rational or reasonable—even if always beyond our full grasp—and it is fundamentally personal. Yet it affirms rather than denies the stark difference between good and evil, the way of truth and the way of error, the kingdom of light and the kingdom of darkness. It affirms both rationality as traditionally understood and a rationality that transcends our reason. Wesley is a good model; he knew how to use a syllogism correctly, and he also knew the limitations of syllogistic reasoning.

It is this conjunctive insight that has helped me think *ecologically* in more recent years. It also helps us in thinking about the Trinity, about the *perichoresis* or mutual "dance" of the Father, Son, and Spirit, the "ecology" of the one Tri-personal God.

Here the much disputed "Wesleyan Quadrilateral," despite its flaws, has been useful, for it reminds us that Wesley does in fact use the tools of reason, insights from tradition, and learnings from experience in interpreting the Bible. The starkly missing element is Wesley's affinity for the created order—"the wisdom of God in creation." Quadrilateral thinking ignores the way the "Book of Nature" functioned in Wesley's theology, increasingly so in his later years. If we are going to use any such geometric construct, we should put Scripture at the center with the four emphases of reason, creation, tradition, and experience as elements dynamically circling and interacting with Scripture.

Like many of you, I have attempted to take a both/and approach with regard to Wesley himself. I consider myself an unapologetic partisan of Wesley and his ministry and theology. But I insist that he is just one voice in the long story of Christian witness and theology. Our dialogue must include many voices, both past and present, both global and local, and across cultures in the ongoing engagement between Scripture and current contextual challenges.

As time goes by, I find myself wanting more and more to be *homo unius libri*, a man of the Bible—more and more immersed in God's great plan of redemption that is so marvelously revealed there. As I continue to apply and expand upon the tools of inductive Bible study that I learned in seminary, I am constantly finding fresh things in Scripture about God's great healing, restoring plan in Jesus Christ (which is the theme of my forthcoming book, *Salvation Means Creation Healed*). At seventy-one, I find renewed excitement in Bible study, particularly in the light of Jesus' incarnation and resurrection and his remarkable hermeneutical instruction: "Search the Scriptures, for they testify of me." Only in recent years have I come to see the absolute centrality of Jesus' physical resurrection in space and time for discerning God's overall plan (*oikonomia*) for "the restoration of all things," the new, renewed earth and heaven.

Over the past few years I've become increasingly convinced of how much of theology comes down to the centrality of Scripture and issues of hermeneutics. I am more and more convinced that the proper standpoint for Christian theology is to inhabit the world of Scripture (to paraphrase Lesslie Newbigin), and above all to interpret the world and all of theology through Jesus' incarnation, life, and resurrection, rather than fitting those central acts of God in time and history into some alien or external framework, whether it is labeled "Wesleyan" or something else.

God still seems to be up to something through Jesus Christ by the Spirit, and it is exciting to be a part of it. And, I believe, we still have much to learn from John Wesley.

SUSIE CUNNINGHAM STANLEY

The tribute by Barry L. Callen, March, 2012.

An awareness of theological differences emerged at sixteen as Susie Cunningham became active in Youth for Christ. She confronted terms like predestination and rapture. YFCers felt free to employ the "heretic" label to describe Susie's Arminianism. Despite the negative label, her peers elected her president of the largest club in Cleveland and president of the Cleveland area officers. Sexism, though, kept her from the position of captain of the Bible quiz team, even though she met the criteria of having the most points. Dealing with these theological differences and sexism prepared Susie for her future commitment to Wesleyan/Holiness theology and biblical feminism. Her experience with these quintessential evangelicals also helps explain her refusal to accept that label for herself.

Susie was a stay-at-home mom when God called her to ministry at an Evangelical Women's Caucus (EWC) conference in 1975. She founded the Michigan chapter of EWC. Also, before seminary, she promoted the Equal Rights Amendment and women's health issues. Susie attended seminary at Iliff School of Theology and did her graduate work in a joint program at Iliff and University of Denver, graduating in 1987.

The Church of God (Anderson) ordained Susie in 1983 as an Ecumenical Minister. She has fulfilled that designation by preaching in Presbyterian, Methodist, Lutheran, Brethren in Christ, and Nazarene congregations. She has even preached and distributed the Eucharist at a Roman Catholic parish. She has conducted workshops at national Seventh Day Adventist, Church of God, and Evangelical Covenant churches and at regional meetings for The Salvation Army, American Baptists, and Mennonites. She has preached at numerous universities and seminaries, including Asbury University, Seattle Pacific University, and Azusa Pacific University. She has delivered lecture series on holiness themes at ten universities or seminaries. And conducted faculty retreats on numerous topics.

In addition to her being a board member of Ecumenical Ministries of Oregon (a national Council of Churches affiliate), a highlight of Stanley's ecumenical involvement was being the Wesleyan/Holiness delegate to the Fifth World Conference on Faith and Order in Spain, sponsored by the World Council of Churches. Who knew that Rowan Williams who shared her sense of humor and whose assigned seat was directly behind hers would become the Archbishop of Canterbury?

Susie began her teaching career at Western Evangelical Seminary (now George Fox Evangelical Seminary) in 1983 and moved to Messiah College in 1995 where she retired in 2011. She taught a variety of courses, primarily theology but also church history, new religious movements, Black theology, women's studies, and practical ministry. She has served as an adjunct professor at seven schools, including Drew, Iliff, Fuller, Canadian Theological Seminary, and Nazarene Theological Seminary. The theme of love permeates her teaching. She began her theology classes with a session on love, incorporating contemporary music, art, crafts, and even heart-shaped candy.

Stanley's involvement in various academic societies reflects her broad interests. She has delivered papers at the Society for the Scientific Study of Religion, the American Society of Church History, the National Women's Studies Association, Berkshire Conference on the History of Women, the Society for Pentecostal Studies and the American Academy of Religion where she also served on the steering committee of two sections and president of the Northwest AAR/SBL. Her research has benefited from grants awarded by Messiah College, the Lilly Foundation, the AAR Collaborative Research Grant, Louisville Institute, Wabash Center, and the Pew Charitable Trust.

In terms of the Wesleyan Theological Society, Stanley's tenure as Society president in 1992-1993 resulted in putting the Society back on strong financial footing and maintaining the journal's reputation by calling Barry L. Callen to the editorship. The idea of a joint meeting of the Society for Pentecostal Studies and the Wesleyan Theological Society had been floating around for some time, but it was Stanley and Cheryl Bridges Johns who issued a call which resulted in the first such meeting.

Stanley authored a biography of Alma White. Her *Holy Boldness: Women's Autobiographies and the Sanctified Self* assessed books by thirty-seven women preachers. She was the primary editor of *Faith and Gender Equity*, consisting of lesson plans promoting equality and designed for general education classes. She has written forty-four articles or book chapters and led numerous workshops and conferences in the United States, Canada, and England. She helped plan the first conference for women in ministry and missions in the Church of God (Anderson). On a larger scale, she founded Wesleyan/Holiness Women Clergy and served as volunteer executive director for fifteen years, working with the seven sponsoring denominations.

THE STANLEY RESPONSE

As we've been reminded today, holiness is relational. I feel that way about this award as well. It wouldn't have been possible without the help of others. Many of you are here in this room. You invited me to speak or teach at your schools. You worked hard to send students to the Wesleyan/Holiness Women Clergy conferences. I know the time it takes to arrange for this—from securing the funds to dealing with all the details involved. Thank you. And a special thanks to my children Mike and Mandy and my highly supportive husband John.

WILLIAM ("Billy") J. ABRAHAM

The tribute by Jason E. Vickers, March, 2013.

A self-described bog-Irish Methodist with an Oxford education and an Eastern Orthodox update, William J. "Billy" Abraham embodies an ecclesial practice historically associated with Methodism itself, namely, itinerancy. Constantly on the move, he is a philosopher, pastor, evangelist, missionary, catechist, and systematic theologian. He is also a keen observer of international politics, a preacher, a Sunday school teacher, a spiritual and theological mentor to students, a distinguished university teaching professor, and a close personal friend to many clergy and professional academics. Those who know him best marvel at his boundless energy for theology and ministry.

Despite the breadth of his scholarly interests and activities, Abraham's work can be mapped along two trajectories. The first trajectory reflects his philosophical interests, as indicated by such titles as *Divine Revelation and the Limits of Historical Criticism* (1982, republished in 2000 as an Oxford Scholarly Classic), *An Introduction to the*

Philosophy of Religion (1985), and most recently, *Crossing the Threshold of Divine Revelation* (2006) and *Aldersgate and Athens: John Wesley and the Foundations of Christian Belief* (2010). This 2010 work is partly a reflection of his own journey from skepticism and philosophical atheism to Christianity.

The second trajectory represents Abraham's engagement with the life of the church, as evidenced by such titles as *The Coming Great Revival: Recovering the Full Evangelical Tradition* (1984), *The Logic of Evangelism* (1989), *The Art of Evangelism: Evangelism Carefully Crafted into the Life of the Local Church* (1993), *Waking from Doctrinal Amnesia* (1995), and *The Logic of Renewal* (2003). For Abraham, the purpose of evangelism and missions is, with the help of the Holy Spirit, to initiate people into the Kingdom of God. As he conceives it, however, the task of initiation requires prolonged and patient catechesis. On this front, Abraham has written basic catechetical materials that have been used in local churches around the world, and regularly preaching and teaching in places as diverse as Costa Rica, Kazakhstan, Malasyia, Nepal, and Romania.

Abraham's mature theological vision brings together these two distinct trajectories of thought. In *Canon and Criterion in Christian Theology: From the Fathers to Feminism* (the recipient of the 2001 Smith-Wynkoop Book Award of the WTS), he set forth and explored an illuminating insight about the difference between ecclesial canons on the one hand and epistemic criteria on the other. Ecclesial canons function within the life of the church as "means of grace and salvation," whereas epistemic criteria are "means of demarcating truth from falsehood, reality from illusion, rationality from irrationality, knowledge from opinion" (1-2). For ordinary Christians, Abraham's work shows that God has given the church an entire range of materials, persons, and practices in and through which the Holy Spirit is present and at work immersing people in the Triune life of God. These include Holy Scripture, doctrine, sacraments, liturgy, episcopal oversight, iconography, and saints. Taken together, these materials, persons and practices comprise the canonical heritage of the church.

Abraham's work has inspired a long-haul research program known as Canonical Theism. His work liberates Christian philosophers and theologians to attend to the vast array of resources and proposals concerning knowledge, truth, rationality, and the justification of religious beliefs that have emerged in religious epistemology over the last twenty-five to thirty years. Instead of shoehorning ecclesial canons into the conversation, Christian philosophers and theologians are free to examine the wide range of options now available with a view toward discerning appropriate epistemic fit with the Christian faith.

The deep motivation behind Abraham's mature theological vision is his abiding concern for church renewal. Above all, Billy Abraham is a renewalist. His commitment to church renewal reflects his early and deep formation in the Methodist theological tradition. To be sure, Abraham frequently draws upon Eastern Orthodox resources, but at no point has he abandoned his Irish Methodist heritage. His ongoing commitment to Methodism can be seen in his regular contributions to Wesleyan and Methodist studies over the last thirty years, including, most recently, *Wesley for Armchair Theologians* (2005), *The Oxford Handbook of Methodist Studies* (2009), and the controversial and often quoted *Wesleyan Theological Journal* essay "The End of Wesleyan Theology" (Fall 2005), in which he makes the case that, instead of perceiving Wesley as a great systematic theologian, Methodists should receive and emulate Wesley as a saint of the church.

However, Abraham's Methodist theological orientation is perhaps best reflected in his commitment to pneumatology as the heart and soul of both Christian theology and the Christian life. Like Wesley himself, Abraham undertakes theological reflection from the standpoint of the third article of the Creed. In good Methodist fashion, he insists that, while the Holy Spirit has given the church an overabundance of gifts for her sustenance and healing, what matters most is our "reception of the Giver of the gifts, the life-giving Holy Spirit who comes to baptize and immerse us into the life of God" (*Canon and Criterion*, 54).

THE ABRAHAM RESPONSE

Within the Wesleyan tradition, it would be fair to say that I have been something of a gadfly, giving the appearance that I am all too ready to pick a quarrel not just with the tradition but with those who have been stalwart and worthy defenders of the tradition. My work within the tradition has been driven by several laudable desires, that is, to read the tradition faithfully, to avoid projecting my own concerns onto the tradition, and to face up to the problems that the tradition has had to tackle across the years, and which it still must face today.

In terms of actual writing within the Wesleyan tradition, one volume that has given me special satisfaction is the *Oxford Handbook of*

Methodist Studies that I co-edited with James Kirby. I tackled there the thorny topic of Christian perfection. I am convinced that this is, as we all know, a crucial part of our heritage. I think the vision developed by John Wesley and the early Methodists still has legs under it. When I started teaching formally in the Outler Chair at Perkins School of Theology, one of my goals was to see to it that Methodist Studies would, at some point, be recognized by Oxford University Press. It is an additional pleasure to see serious engagement with our tradition now being picked up by Cambridge University Press because of the fine editorial work by Randy Maddox and Jason Vickers.

We belong to a noble stream of the Christian tradition. As Donald Dayton has long insisted, we represent a post-Reformation tradition that reaches back into the Christian past and forward into the tumultuous world of Pentecostalism. In fact, I think that Wesley re-read the early patristic period in the light of his experience in revival and awakening; this deserves further attention in the years ahead. This whole trajectory of faith and practice we have inherited from Wesley deserves to be represented at the highest levels of the academy and at the forefront of Christian social and missionary practice. I will begin from below with divine action in the Christian life. I have no qualms about being a Supernaturalist and a Pietist of a lower order! I thank you one and all!

Thomas Jay Oord, Jürgen Moltmann, and Amos Yong

Steven McCormick and Steven Gunter

Michael Lodahl and Albert Truesdale

Appendix A
WTS Leaders: Presidents and Editors

Key elected leaders of the Wesleyan Theological Society have been those chosen to serve as the President of the Society and the Editor of the Society's academic publication, the *Wesleyan Theological Journal*. Following are those persons and their terms of service.

EDITORS OF THE
WESLEYAN THEOLOGICAL JOURNAL

Charles W. Carter, 1965-1972
Harvey J. S. Blaney, 1973
W. T. Purkiser, 1974-1975
Leon O. Hynson, 1976-1978
Lee M. Haines, 1979-1981
Alex R. G. Deasley, 1982-1986
Paul M. Bassett, 1987-1992
Barry L. Callen, 1993-2014
Jason E. Vickers, 2015 to present

PRESIDENTS OF THE
WESLEYAN THEOLOGICAL SOCIETY

Leo Cox, 1965
Richard S. Taylor, 1965-66
William M. Arnett, 1966-67
Lowell Roberts, 1967-68
Merne A. Harris, 1968-69
Ralph E. Perry, 1969-70
Robert A. Mattke, 1970-71
George H. Blackstone, 1971-72
Robert A. Mattke, 1972-73
Delbert R. Rose, 1973-74
Mildred B. Wynkoop, 1974-75
Rob Staples, 1975-76
W. Ralph Thompson, 1976-77
Melvin E. Dieter, 1977-78
John A. Knight, 1978-79
Laurence W. Wood, 1979-1980
Wayne G. McCown, 1980-81
Paul M. Bassett, 1981-1982
David L. Thompson, 1982-83
David L. Cubie, 1983-84
R. Larry Shelton, 1984-85
H. Ray Dunning, 1985-86
Frank G. Carver, 1986-87
Howard E. Snyder, 1987-88
Luke L. Keefer, 1988-89
Donald W. Dayton, 1989-90
Randy L. Maddox, 1990-91
W. Stephen Gunter, 1991-92
Susie C. Stanley, 1992-93
George Lyons, 1993-94
Donald A. D. Thorsen, 1994-95
Kenneth J. Collins, 1995-96
Wesley D. Tracy, 1996-97
Douglas M. Strong, 1997-99
Albert L. Truesdale, 1999-2000
Steven McCormick, 2000-01
Sharon Clark Pearson, 2001-02
David Bundy, 2002-03
Henry H. Knight III, 2003-04
Philip R. Meadows, 2004-05
Craig Keen, 2005-06
Carl C. Campbell, 2006-07
Diane Leclerc, 2007-08
Thomas Jay Oord, 2008-09
Thomas Noble, 2009-10
Rob Wall, 2010-11

Elaine Heath, 2011-12
Michael Lodahl, 2012-13
Jason E. Vickers, 2013-14
Richard Thompson, 2014-15
Doug Koskela, 2015-16

D. William Faupel and James Earl Massey

Stanley Ingersol and Charles Edwin Jones

Appendix B

Host Institutions for WTS Annual Meetings

It has been the practice of the Wesleyan Theological Society to convene its annual meetings on the campuses of institutions of higher education that have historic ties with Wesleyan/Holiness/Pentecostal traditions of Christianity. The purposes of this practice have been (1) to strengthen such ties and (2) to acquaint Society members more directly with this wide range of institutions. The following campuses have hosted one or more WTS annual meetings.

Anderson University School of Theology, IN
Asbury Theological Seminary, KY
Ashland Theological Seminary, OH
Azusa Pacific University, CA
Bethel College, IN
Church of God Theological Seminary, TN
Duke Divinity School, NC
Emory University (Candler SOT), GA
Evangelical School of Theology, PA
Hobe Sound Bible College, FL
Huntington University, IN
Indiana Wesleyan University, IN
Mt. Vernon Nazarene University, OH
Nazarene Bible College, CO
Nazarene Theological Seminary, MO
Northwest Nazarene University, ID
Olivet Nazarene University, IL
Ohio Christian University (Circleville), OH
Point Loma Nazarene University, CA
Roberts Wesleyan College, NY
Seattle Pacific University, WA
Southern Methodist University (Perkins), TX
Southern Nazarene University, OK
Spring Arbor University, MI
Trevecca Nazarene University, TN

United Theological Seminary, OH
Wesley Theological Seminary, Wash., D.C.
Western Evangelical Seminary, OR

Appendix C
The Smith/Wynkoop Book Award

The annual book award given by the Wesleyan Theological Society is named in honor of the outstanding scholarly contributions of historian Timothy L. Smith and theologian Mildred Bangs Wynkoop. It is given in order to recognize a recent publication of distinction in a research area related to the Wesleyan/Holiness tradition. Each book honored is judged to have helped this particular Christian tradition to be better understood and/or promoted. Listed below are the recipients.

2000. **Douglas M. Strong**. Perfectionist Politics: Abolitionism and the Religious Tensions of American Democracy. Syracuse University Press. 1999.

2001. **William J. Abraham**. Canon and Criterion in Christian Theology. Clarendon Press Oxford. 1998.

2002. **Diane Leclerc**. Singleness of Heart: Gender, Sin, and Holiness in Historical Perspective. The Scarecrow Press. 2001.

2003. **Laurence W. Wood**. The Meaning of Pentecost in Early Methodism. The Scarecrow Press. 2002.

2004. **Floyd Cunningham**. *Holiness Abroad: Nazarene Missions in Asia*. Scarecrow Press. 2003.

2005. **Samuel M. Powell**. *Participating in God: Creation and Trinity*. Fortress Press. 2003.

2006. **James Earl Massey**. African Americans and the Church of God: Aspects of a Social *History*. Anderson University Press. 2005.

2007. **Howard A. Snyder**. Populist Saints: B. T. and Ellen Roberts and the First Free Methodists. William B. Eerdmans Publishing. 2006.

2008. **Charles Edwin Jones**. Comprehensive Bibliographic Guides to the Holiness, Keswick, and Charismatic Movements (3 vols., various years).

2009. **Randall J. Stephens**. The Fire Spreads: Holiness and Pentecostalism in the American South. Harvard University Press, 2008.

2010. **Randy L. Maddox and Jason E. Vickers**, eds. *The Cambridge Companion to John Wesley.* Cambridge, 2010.
2011. **John Wigger.** *American Saint: Francis Asbury & the Methodists.* Oxford Univ. Press, 2009.
2012. **Dean Flemming**, *Philippians: A Commentary in the Wesleyan Tradition.* Beaco Hill Press of Kansas City, 2009.
2013. (None awarded)
2014. **Robert W. Wall**, *1 & 2 Timothy and Titus.* Eerdmans, 2012.

Barry L. Callen and Howard A. Snyder

Appendix D

Archived WTS Materials

by Steven Hoskins

The Archives of the Wesleyan Theological Society (WTS) is held in the Archives, Rare Books, and Special Collections of The David Allan Hubbard Library of Fuller Theological Seminary. It includes 20 boxes with over 16 linear feet of correspondence, organizational documents, minutes, membership records, audio tapes, microfilms, and conference papers of the Society's fifty-year history, along with a full run of the *Wesleyan Theological Journal*, the official publication of the WTS.

Among the archival holdings are several significant documents relating to the earliest years of the WTS. Particularly noteworthy are papers from meetings which predated the formal beginning of the Society, collected and published as *Insights into Holiness* (1963) and *Further Insights into Holiness* (1963). These conferences culminated in the Winona Lake Study Conference on the "Distinctives of Arminian-Wesleyan Theology," held in November, 1964, and sponsored by the National Holiness Association. Papers from this conference were published as *The Word and the Doctrine* in 1965 and are included in the collection as well. It was this meeting that set the stage for the organization of the Wesleyan Theological Society at the April, 1965, NHA meeting in Detroit.

Other valuable documents relating to the early history of the WTS include the extensive correspondence of Rev. Thomas Hersey (1965-1982), an original member of the Society and a Methodist minister in Iowa. Original correspondence concerning the establishing of the Society is from early WTS officers and other leaders, such as Kenneth

Geiger, Wilbur Dayton, Wayne Caldwell, Melvin Dieter, and Charles W. Carter. A November, 1970, letter concerning the fundamentalist controversy between the Society and its parent body, the NHA, is by Charles Carter, at that time chair of the WTS Editorial Committee. It does much to explain that debate and the Society's decision to amend its bylaws to reflect a "dynamic plenary inspiration" understanding of Scripture.

The highlight of the collection is a complete set of annual meeting programs, listing the host institutions and all paper writers and titles. The collection also holds the original constitution of the Society as adopted in 1969, with revisions to that constitution in handwriting in 1978, minutes of the annual meetings, officers reports, membership reports, membership applications prior to 1991, reports of the WTS liaisons to the Faith & Order Commission of the National Council of Churches, the Wesleyan Holiness Study Project (1987), the reports of the liaison to Wesleyan/Holiness Women Clergy (2002-2003), and some audio cassettes of papers given at conferences in the 1970s. Documents relating to international meetings held with the Bahamas Wesleyan Fellowship (2003) and a joint conference with Seoul Theological University in Seoul, South Korea (2007) are included in the archives as well. A three-page listing of the actions taken by the membership from 1965-1977 provides excellent insight into the dynamics of the Society at its earliest meetings.

The archives also holds records of the Society's numerous ecumenical endeavors, most notably joint meetings with the Society for Pentecostal Studies (SPS). SPS hosted the first joint meeting at the Church of God Theological Seminary in Cleveland, TN, in 1998. A full record of the papers presented at that meeting are included. Building on the success of that meeting, a second joint WTS-SPS meeting was hosted in 2003 by the Wesleyan/Holiness Studies Center of Asbury Theological Seminary. A third joint meeting was held at Duke University Divinity School in 2008, and most recently at Seattle Pacific University in 2013. Records of the programs for each of these meetings are included in the holdings.

Portions of the archives will be available to researchers fully digitized and online in 2015 thanks to an agreement between the David Allan Hubbard Library at Fuller Seminary and the Duke University Divinity School Library. These digitized holdings will be included in the several archival collections related to the history of American Methodism and will be found at http://divintyarchive.com/. A link to the collection can also be found on the Society's website at www.wtsweb.org. Thanks from the WTS goes to Adam Gossman, Fuller Library archivist, and Beth Shepherd, Duke Divinity archivist, for bringing this project to fruition. Permission to use the collection for academic research and publication can be obtained by application to the Promotional Secretary of the WTS.

Appendix E

Recent WTS Annual Meetings With Host Institutions and Meeting Themes

The second issue of the *Wesleyan Theological Journal* following each annual meeting of the WTS has typically focused on that meeting's theme and featured select papers presented there.

Years	Host Institutions	Annual Meeting Themes
1991	Western Evangelical Seminary, Oregon	Gospel for the Poor
1992	Ashland Theological Seminary, Ohio	Wesleyanism and Modernity
1993	Southern Nazarene University, Oklahoma	Wesleyanism and Eschatology
1994	United Theological Seminary, Ohio	Asserting Our Biblical Heritage
1995	Northwest Nazarene University, Idaho	Sanctification and New Creation
1996	Wesley Theological Seminary, Wash. D.C.	The Worship of God
1997	Mount Vernon Nazarene University, Ohio	Facing the Future
1998	Church of God Seminary, Tennessee Joint with the Society for Pentecostal Studies	Purity and Power
1999	Southern Nazarene University, Oklahoma	Wesleyanism and the Postmodern Age
2000	Azusa Pacific University, California	The Holy Trinity
2001	Indiana Wesleyan University, Indiana	Power and Reconciliation
2002	Hobe Sound Bible College, Florida	Mission in the Wesleyan Traditions
2003	Asbury Theological Seminary, Kentucky Joint with the Society for Pentecostal Studies	Wesleyan and Pentecostal Movements for a New Century
2004	Roberts Wesleyan College, New York	Practicing Our Wesleyan Theology
2005	Seattle Pacific University, Washington	The Church—the Body of Christ
2006	Nazarene Theological Seminary, Missouri	Friendship and Hospitality
2007	Olivet Nazarene University, Illinois	Suffering and the Holy Life
2008	School of Divinity, Duke Univ., North Carolina Joint with the Society for Pentecostal Studies	Science and Creation
2009	Anderson University, Indiana	The Centrality of Christ
2010	Azusa Pacific University, California	The Future of Scripture
2011	Perkins School of Theology, SMU, Texas	Empire, Church, and *Missio Dei*
2012	Travecca Nazarene University, Tennessee	Wesleyanism and World Religions
2013	Seattle Pacific University, Washington Joint with the Society for Pentecostal Studies	Holiness
2014	Northwest Nazarene University, Idaho	Atonement in the Wesleyan Tradition
2015	Mount Vernon Nazarene University, Ohio	The Past and Future of Wesleyan-Holiness Identity

Index of Names

Abbott, H. Mark, 41
Abraham, William J., 32, 34,
    39, 105, 114-117, 125
Agnew, Milton S., 18, 20
Alchin, Canon, 25
Arias, Mortimer, 3, 25
Arnett, William M., 2, 17,
    43, 120
Baker, Frank, 3, 43, 48
Bangs, Carl, 94
Bassett, Paul M., 30, 44,
    51, 59, 69, 73, 77, 93-95,
    119-120
Bauer, David R., 62
Blackstone, George H., 2, 120
Blaising, Craig, 3, 25
Blaney, Harvey J. S., 44, 119
Boone, Dan, 41
Borger, Steven, 41
Branson, Robert, 41
Bridges Johns, Cheryl, 31, 113
Brown, Dale, 3, 25
Brueggemann, Walter, 39
Bundy, David, 33-34, 44, 81,
    83, 120
Caldwell, Wayne, 128
Callen, Barry L., iii, vi,
    30-31, 33-34, 40, 43-44,
    46, 48-49, 61, 66, 99-101,
    111, 119, 126
Calvin, John, 24, 49
Campbell, Carl C., 33, 42,
    60, 120
Caputo, John, 41
Carter, Charles W., 2, 8, 13-14,

18, 44, 119, 128
Cartwright, Michael, 39
Carver, Frank G., 120
Childs, Brevard, 64
Clark, Brian, 40
Climenhaga, Arthur M., 18, 44
Collins, Kenneth J., 22, 30, 120
Cox, Leo G., iii, vi, 2, 5, 17-18,
    43-44, 120
Cruickshank, Joanne, 40
Cubie, David L., 120
Cunningham, Floyd, 34, 125
Dayton, Donald W., iii, vi, 3, 11,
    18-19, 25, 36, 53, 81,
    102-105, 117, 120
Dayton, Wilber T., 17-19,
    43-44, 128
Deasley, Alex R. G., 44, 119
Dieter, Melvin E., 12, 30, 51,
    69-71, 86, 120, 128
Duncan, Ronald V., 41
Dunning, H. Ray, 34, 73,
    90, 120
Eby, Patrick Alan, 40
Faupel, D. William, 31, 44,
    81, 122
Flemming, Dean, 126
Fuhrman, Eldon, 3, 19
Gause, R. Hollis, 31
Geiger, Kenneth E., 20, 44,
    127-128
Greathouse, William M., 31, 72
Grider, J. Kenneth, 1, 6, 32, 77
Gunter, W. Stephen, 98,
    118, 120
Haines, Lee M., 44, 119
Hammond, Geordan, 40
Harris, Merne A., 2, 6-7, 17, 43
Hartley, Benjamin L., 40
Hauerwas, Stanley, 35, 39
Heath, Elaine, 39, 42, 121

Hersey, Thomas, 127
Hoskins, Steven, iii, vi, 37, 127
Hynson, Leon O., 44, 119
Ingersol, Stanley, 44, 93, 122
Jennings, Theodore, 25
Johnston, Robert K., 103
Jones, Charles Edwin, 34, 89, 122, 125
Keefer, Luke L., 120
Keen, Craig, 42, 90, 98, 120
King, Martin Luther, Jr., 66
Kinghorn, Kenneth, 3, 35, 44
Kinsey, Andrew, 41
Kirby, James, 117
Knight, Henry H. III, 34, 120
Knight, John A., 120
Koskela, Doug, 121
Koskie, Steven Joe, 40
Kostlevy, William, iii, 1, 35, 46, 80
Leclerc, Diane, 42, 59, 98, 120, 125
Lewis, C. S., 57
Lodahl, Michael, 42, 57, 118, 121
Logan, J. Sutherland, 8
Luhn, Robert, 41
Luther, Martin, 49
Lyons, George, 24, 30, 120
McCormack, Bruce, 39
McCormick, Steven, 33, 96, 98, 118, 120
McCown, Wayne G., 120
McGonigle, Herbert, 13, 46
McKenna, David L., 33, 83-85
McPheeters, J. C., 1
Maddox, Randy L., 28, 39, 46, 98, 117, 120, 126
Mahan, Asa, 13
Mann, Mark H., 40
Marshall, I. Howard, 39

Marty, Martin, 98
Massey, James Earl, 30,
   66-69, 122, 125
Mattke, Robert A., 2, 8, 120
Meadows, Philip R., 35,
   55, 120
Mercer, Jerry, 3, 35
Merritt, John G., iii, vi, 17, 21
Moltmann, Jürgen, 39, 117
Montgomery, Brint, 32
Muhammad, 57
Noble, Thomas, 42, 56, 120
Oden, Thomas, 3
Oord, Thomas Jay, 32, 34,
   41-42, 98, 117, 120
Outler, Albert, 3, 15
Park, Myung Soo, 35
Pearson, Sharon Clark, 33, 120
Peisker, Armor D., 18, 44
Perry, Ralph E., 2, 120
Peterson, Brent D., 40
Petry, Ray, 94
Pinnock, Clark H., 31, 100
Pohl, Christine, 39
Postlewait, Brian, 40
Powell, Samuel, 35, 41, 125
Purkiser, W. T., 44, 119
Roberts, Lowell, 2, 120
Robertson, Frederick W., 108
Rodes, Stanley J., 40
Rose, Delbert R., 2, 5, 32,
   80-82, 104, 120
Rose, Susan A. Schultz, 32,
   80-81, 104
Rowell, Jeren, 40-41
Scott, Lane, 36
Seamands, David A., 31, 74-76
Seamands, Stephen A., 74
Schultz, Susan—see Rose
Shade, Major JoAnn, 41
Shelton, R. Larry, 120

Smith, Joseph H., 81-82
Smith, Timothy L., 3, 13,
    32, 70, 105, 125
Snyder, Howard A., iii, vi, 23,
    106-110, 120, 125, 126
Stanger, Frank, 6, 63
Stanley, John, 113
Stanley, Susie C., 30-31,
    111-113, 120
Staples, Rob L., 72, 96, 120
Stephens, Randall J., 125
Strong, Douglas M., 28, 32,
    120, 125
Synan, Vinson, 14, 105
Tait, Jennifer Woodruff, iii,
    vi, 29
Taylor, A. Wingrove, 33, 86-88
Taylor, Richard S., 2, 7,
    35-36, 92, 120
Thompson, David L., 120
Thompson, Frank, 12
Thompson, Richard P., 42, 44,
    99-100, 121
Thompson, Robert, 32
Thompson, W. Ralph, 2, 7, 9,
    17, 43-44, 120
Thorsen, Donald A. D., 30,
    36, 54, 102, 120
Tracy, Wesley D., 31, 120
Traina, Robert A., 30, 62
Truesdale, Albert L., 32,
    118, 120
Turner, George, 12, 45
Vickers, Jason E., 42, 44, 114,
    117, 119, 121, 126
Volf, Miroslav, 39
Wall, Robert W., 42, 120, 126
Warner, Daniel S., 100
Watty, William, 41
Wesley, John, 2, 5, 18-21,
    26, 33, 38, 47-50, 53, 55,

57-58, 97, 107-108
White, Alma, 113
White, Stephen Solomon, 78
White, Wilbert Webster, 63
Wigger, John, 126
Wood, Laurence W., vi, 22, 34, 46, 120, 125
Wright, N. T., 57
Wynkoop, Mildred B., 2, 32, 46, 49, 73, 120, 125
Yoder, John Howard, 3, 15, 47
Yong, Amos, 39, 117
Young, Frances M., 39

www.ingramcontent.com/pod-product-compliance
Lightning Source LLC
Chambersburg PA
CBHW021812220426
43662CB00006B/280